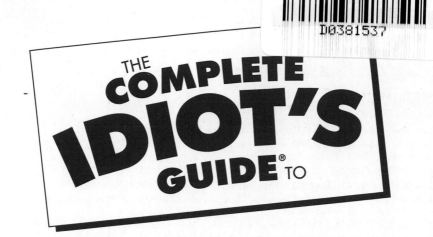

THE COMPLETE IDIOT'S GUIDE® TO

Recovering from Identity Theft

by Mari J. Frank

ALPHA

A member of Penguin Group (USA) Inc.

This book is dedicated to the memory of my mother, Sondra Bear. I wish she had been around as I wrote this book to interject her wonderful wisdom and humor.

ALPHA BOOKS

Published by the Penguin Group

Penguin Group (USA) Inc., 375 Hudson Street, New York, New York 10014, USA

Penguin Group (Canada), 90 Eglinton Avenue East, Suite 700, Toronto, Ontario M4P 2Y3, Canada (a division of Pearson Penguin Canada Inc.)

Penguin Books Ltd., 80 Strand, London WC2R 0RL, England

Penguin Ireland, 25 St. Stephen's Green, Dublin 2, Ireland (a division of Penguin Books Ltd.)

Penguin Group (Australia), 250 Camberwell Road, Camberwell, Victoria 3124, Australia (a division of Pearson Australia Group Pty. Ltd.)

Penguin Books India Pvt. Ltd., 11 Community Centre, Panchsheel Park, New Delhi—110 017, India

Penguin Group (NZ), 67 Apollo Drive, Rosedale, North Shore, Auckland 1311, New Zealand (a division of Pearson New Zealand Ltd.)

Penguin Books (South Africa) (Pty.) Ltd., 24 Sturdee Avenue, Rosebank, Johannesburg 2196, South Africa

Penguin Books Ltd., Registered Offices: 80 Strand, London WC2R 0RL, England

International Standard Book Number: 978-1-59257-992-1
Library of Congress Catalog Card Number: 2009938584

12 11 10   8 7 6 5 4 3 2 1

Interpretation of the printing code: The rightmost number of the first series of numbers is the year of the book's printing; the rightmost number of the second series of numbers is the number of the book's printing. For example, a printing code of 10-1 shows that the first printing occurred in 2010.

Printed in the United States of America

Note: This publication contains the opinions and ideas of its author. It is intended to provide helpful and informative material on the subject matter covered. It is sold with the understanding that the author and publisher are not engaged in rendering professional services in the book. If the reader requires personal assistance or advice, a competent professional should be consulted.

The author and publisher specifically disclaim any responsibility for any liability, loss, or risk, personal or otherwise, which is incurred as a consequence, directly or indirectly, of the use and application of any of the contents of this book.

Most Alpha books are available at special quantity discounts for bulk purchases for sales promotions, premiums, fund-raising, or educational use. Special books, or book excerpts, can also be created to fit specific needs.

For details, write: Special Markets, Alpha Books, 375 Hudson Street, New York, NY 10014.

Publisher: *Marie Butler-Knight*
Editorial Director: *Mike Sanders*
Senior Managing Editor: *Billy Fields*
Acquisitions Editor: *Karyn Gerhard*
Senior Development Editor: *Phil Kitchel*
Senior Production Editor: *Megan Douglass*

Cover Designer: *Bill Thomas*
Book Designer: *Trina Wurst*
Indexer: *Brad Herriman*
Layout: *Ayanna Lacey*
Proofreader: *John Etchison*

Contents at a Glance

Contents

Foreword

When I became the director of the State of California Office of Privacy Protection upon its opening in 2001, I knew I needed to get advice from the experts. Mari Frank was one of the first professionals I turned to in setting up an advisory committee. Mari was part of the small group of consumer advocates, business people, and attorneys knowledgeable about privacy who helped me to set the agenda for the very first in the nation Office of Privacy Protection. She has been helpful to the office in many ways over the years. When we developed our various "Recommended Practices" white papers on protecting Social Security numbers, on information-sharing disclosures and privacy policy statements, and on responding to privacy breaches, which were intended to encourage businesses and other entities to adopt policies and practices that respect individual privacy, Mari was there to review drafts and provide valuable suggestions. When California held major summits on identity theft and security in various cities in the state to educate consumers and businesses on privacy practices and identity-theft protections, Mari was there for the Office of Privacy Protection as a presenter to share her expertise—always to rave reviews.

From the beginning, Mari was one of those who insisted we put identity theft at the top of our agenda, where it has remained to this day. More than half of the calls and e-mails we get at the California Office of Privacy Protection are about identity theft. We hear from upset people who've just learned they are victims, from frustrated victims who have been running into brick walls in trying to undo the mess, and from concerned consumers who simply fear they might become victims. On occasion, we have asked Mari to help some of the most challenged victims, and she has given generously of her time to assist them at no cost.

Over the years, victims have gained more legal rights and redress tools, but the problem of identity theft has persisted. It has in fact become more complicated, more varied, and more pernicious. No longer a "crime of convenience" perpetrated by acquaintances or others with ready access to our credit or bank account information, identity theft is now a tool of organized crime, part of elaborate international criminal schemes to steal data.

That's why Mari's book is so important. While the crime of identity theft is often complicated, its consumer victims need plain-language, easy-to-use instructions to recover from it. Mari's personal experience as a former identity-theft victim makes her very sensitive to the difficulties involved. Even more important, her skills as a lawyer and privacy expert enable her to add real punch to the various tools and guidance she provides in this book. Educating and empowering consumers has been Mari's objective for as long as I have known her as a lawyer, professor, and radio host, and it is also essential to accomplishing the mission of the California Office of Privacy Protection. Consumers who benefit from using this book will not only be able to help themselves to regain their own identity, but they will also be armed to assist others to do battle in the ongoing fight against identity theft.

—Joanne McNabb, Certified Information Privacy Professional, Government Chief, State of California Office of Privacy Protection

Introduction

Identity theft is the fastest-growing crime in our nation. Estimates from the Federal Trade Commission and other reputable research institutes indicate there are anywhere from 9 to 15 million new victims every year.

Identity thieves can obtain credit cards and loans in your name, get mortgages or apartments using your good credit, substitute their medical histories for yours while committing medical identity theft, get work using your Social Security number, drain your bank accounts, impersonate you on social networking websites, bring the wrath of the IRS down on you, or get you arrested for their criminal deeds. Savvy impostors set up entire businesses as though they are you, and when they take off with customers' monies without fulfilling orders, you are left to answer to furious customers. Even your children and your deceased loved ones are vulnerable to the activities of identity vultures.

Companies and even government agencies have been terribly ineffective at doing the basic identity checks that would stop most fraud in its tracks. For example, thieves can apply for credit cards online with your personal information and never have to present proof of identity. Systems are lax, employees untrained or careless in identity security, and many organizations have decided that it is more profitable to issue credit to criminals and write off the fraud as bad debt than to prevent the problem proactively. When victims contact the entities that fell for the hoaxes, the fraud department investigators are often insensitive and very suspicious of the victims. Unfortunately, inside investigators are often rewarded for denying a fraud claim in order to collect on the account, so they cause increased anguish and re-victimize the victims by forcing them to experience great frustration to overcome enormous obstacles to regain their good name.

There is so much identifying information available about all of us in myriad commercial and governmental databases that criminals find it easy to get the facts necessary to impersonate us. Within the workplace, where a majority of identities are stolen, careless employees lose unencrypted laptops or backup tapes; unscrupulous tempted employees easily sneak out confidential electronic files on minute electronic devices; and hackers break into computer systems to access and sell sensitive data to identity thieves. It's also simple for potential impostors to legally go through unshredded commercial trash bins; or rifle through the local garbage dump searching for valuable data; or, for a small fee, purchase vast profiles about you and your family from commercial information brokers. Consider all the commercial and governmental entities that collect every detail of your life online and offline and store the information in unprotected computer files.

Although recovery won't necessarily be as quick and effortless as you might wish, the good news is that I will be your guide and show you how to be successful in dealing with the toughest of situations. Fortunately, since 1996 when I was victimized myself, we have passed many new laws and have seen major improvements in victim recovery.

Unfortunately, the number of victims has increased each year, and the types of identity theft have expanded. Although new legislation has been passed, the crime has morphed and the laws have not always kept up with the ingenious criminal creativity. The challenge for most consumers, and even businesses as well, is understanding victim legal rights and obligations and the requirements to emerge victoriously from identity theft. And it's even trickier for victims to deal with those instances where current law doesn't suffice to help them remedy certain types of identity theft like cyber identity theft and medical identity theft.

How to Use This Book

My hope is that you will use this book as your coach to lead you effectively through your trials and tribulations to recover completely from this crime. I will provide you with the tools and know-how to deal with virtually any type of identity theft.

You'll learn how to create an effective, logical, step-by-step process to successfully clear your name. I'll show you how to get organized and help you save time. You'll understand the types of information that you need to overcome the arguments and objections of companies and agencies; you'll learn techniques to get the best help from law enforcement; you'll find out how to investigate facts to get entities to understand your needs; you'll be able to challenge the inaccurate information on your consumer and credit reports; you'll be able to assertively deal with intimidating government organizations; and you'll also learn how to access additional resources when you need them most. I've also included a glossary of terms and valuable resources that will help you.

Using this book is similar to reading a travel book, because you might want to pick the chapters and prioritize by what fits your needs. Identity-theft recovery can be like a jigsaw puzzle: you get one piece of evidence, and then find out new facts that affect the next actions to take. To make your learning process easier, I have separated information in individual chapters clarifying what you need to do as you gather new information. For example, you may learn some information from one company that leads you to details that prove fraud for another company or governmental entity. I'll show you how to move easily from one type of identity theft in one chapter to other corresponding types of fraud in other chapters so that you can link the details together and save time and energy resolving the problems with several entities at the same time. Here's how I've divided this guide book into several parts:

Part 1, "First Steps," tells you what every identity-theft victim needs to do.

Part 2, "Restore Your Finances," offers techniques to clear your name with creditors, lenders, banks, insurance companies, and other credit issuers.

Part 3, "The Innocent and Betrayals," tells you how to handle identity theft when children or the deceased are victims, or when friends or relatives take your identity.

Part 4, "Square Away the Bureaucracies," helps you deal with government agencies, your employer, or medical providers.

Part 5, "Where the Going Gets Tough," is for those who find themselves the subject of criminal investigation, a lawsuit, or impersonation online. There is also a chapter on what to do when the process doesn't work smoothly and what else you should do to protect yourself after the recovery process is well underway.

To be most efficient, start your identity recovery by carefully going through the first part of the book in order. This gives you the basics for your ongoing efforts. Next, go to Chapter 4, which teaches you how to obtain, understand, and challenge your credit and consumer reports. You should also check out Chapter 12, to be sure that your Social Security number is secure.

What you read next depends on your particular case. Because almost 80 percent of identity theft is some aspect of financial fraud, chances are you'll need other chapters in Part 2. But you may find yourself skipping to Chapter 14 for medical identity theft or maybe Chapter 13 if someone is trying to do business using your name and credentials.

Hopefully you won't run into too many roadblocks when trying to clear yourself, but if you do, Chapter 18 has many tips on how to get people to listen and when to bring in professional help. And do check Chapter 19, which helps you know how to handle court issues if the identity thief is actually captured and prosecuted. Finally, you'll need to take precautions to keep your identity from being stolen again.

Appendix A has a list of specific terms, and Appendix B has a list of resources that can help you in your efforts, including non-profit, commercial, and federal websites with worthwhile information.

Throughout the book, you'll find special sidebars with additional information. There are four types.

Information = Power

These are useful bits of information that will make the recovery process go more smoothly.

Identity Crisis

These let you know what to look out for in terms of potential problems so you can head them off before they happen.

Legal Lingo

These explain key terms, which also appear in Appendix A, the glossary.

Hidden Agenda

These are important pieces of information about identity theft and recovery.

My purpose in writing this book was to give you the know-how and confidence to regain your credit, your finances, your overall identity, and your good reputation. Although I am a licensed attorney, this book is not legal advice. I have given you legal and consumer information that will empower you to take the necessary steps to recover your identity. But please know that, because I can't address all the possible factual situations that you may experience, and laws are changing all the time, you may need legal assistance. I suggest that you consult with a lawyer in your state for legal advice about your specific circumstances. To find the right professional, call your local county bar association to help you find a specialist who handles identity-theft issues.

By the time you finish reading this book, I hope you'll feel relieved to know that you have moved past your current crises. You'll look back at your accomplishments and feel gratified that you've become wiser and stronger and have overcome many challenging situations. But best of all, you'll regain your good name, recover your identity, and return peace and order to your life.

Acknowledgments

The gift of gratitude is a blessing in life, especially for the one giving thanks. I am delighted to thank the wonderful people who have helped to get this book into your hands. First, I must acknowledge my appreciation for my fabulous literary agent, Marilyn Allen, from Allen-O'Shea Literary Agency. When I received the call from Marilyn asking me to write this book, I was honored and thrilled—until I learned of the short timeline to get it written. But with her encouragement, support, and great sense of humor, she motivated me to persevere through the project. I cannot speak highly enough of the Allen-O'Shea literary agency for its expertise, professionalism, and wonderful encouragement.

Marilyn introduced me to Erik Sherman, a prize-winning independent journalist and author who had worked on several other *Complete Idiot's Guides*. He led me through the process as an editor, and kicked me in the butt to finish each chapter in a timely manner. I am grateful to Erik for his great organization, journalistic prowess, and editing skills. He became my confidant and mentor. I'm sure Erik learned more about identity theft than he ever wanted to!

There are so many terrific folks at Alpha that worked up front and behind the scenes, and I am very grateful to them all for their terrific efforts. First, I thank Karyn Gerhard, my wonderful acquisitions editor, who believed enough in the project to push forward and help me understand what was needed to make this book possible. I especially want to thank Katherine McKim, who spent many hours getting the contract issues straightened out. I know it is never easy to negotiate a contract when you have an attorney on the other side, but she collaborated with me until we made it work for all of us. My gratitude also goes to our development editor, Phil Kitchel, who spent hours helping us to make this book clear, concise, and easy to read. Thank you as well to Marie Butler-Knight, our publisher, who had the vision to put forth this work, and the many other helpful *Complete Idiot's Guides*. I want to thank all those who worked so diligently at Alpha.

I send a very special thank you to Joanne McNabb, Chief of the California Office of Privacy Protection, who was so wonderful to write the foreword to this book. She has not only been a leader in privacy in California, but she is an expert on privacy protection at the federal level as a member of the Homeland Security Privacy Committee. She has been a guiding light for California and the nation with regard to information privacy ethics. I am grateful to her for her fabulous work, her continual collaboration, and her enduring friendship.

My appreciation goes out to my friends Beth Givens, the Director of the Privacy Rights Clearinghouse, and Linda and Jay Foley, the co-founders and co-directors of the Identity Theft Resource Center, who have been wonderful colleagues in the quest for privacy protection and advocacy for identity-theft victims. We have collaborated together for many years, and I honor them for all the work they do for consumer victims of identity theft. I especially want to thank Linda Foley, who gave her time and energy to review this book before it was published to give me valuable feedback and suggestions. I value her insights and our long–term friendship.

A very special note of appreciation goes to Amanda Thatcher, my brilliant executive assistant and paralegal, who serves as my right arm. She is not only a great organizer and PR person, but she's a wise woman and a trusted friend. She kept me in line on this project.

I'm so grateful to my terrific daughter, Alyssa Frank, who aside from her busy schedule as a University of California student, works for me in my law office, and has spent many hours helping me edit, revise, and laugh. To my son, Bryan, my brilliant MBA executive, who calls me between his travels from New York to Chicago; I send a hug for his encouragement. I give special cuddles and a pat on the head to my gorgeous Golden Retriever, Raido, who sat under my feet at my desk and reminded me to take "ear-scratching" and "walking" breaks away from the computer. And of course, I am indebted to my loving husband, Lloyd Boshaw Jr., who many a night brought me dinner as I burned the midnight oil and pounded away at my keyboard. I also send my gratitude to my wonderful clients as well as the many victims who have called me to share their hearts, souls, and stories with me. It was gratifying to watch them recover, gain wisdom, and be empowered by the tools I gave them to regain their identities.

Last, but not least, I thank you, for taking the time to read this book and giving me the gift of helping you to overcome your identity-theft challenges.

Trademarks

All terms mentioned in this book that are known to be or are suspected of being trademarks or service marks have been appropriately capitalized. Alpha Books and Penguin Group (USA) Inc. cannot attest to the accuracy of this information. Use of a term in this book should not be regarded as affecting the validity of any trademark or service mark.

Part 1

First Steps

The first steps are critical in effectively challenging the fraudulent information currently attached to your name. You will learn the signs of identity theft and your legal rights. Organization and effective communication will empower you to recover your identity quickly and smoothly. Once you get the important documentation, you will need to demonstrate your innocence. But don't worry—you will learn how to identify telltale signs of identity theft once you understand the scope of your problem and acquire the know-how to show that you have been victimized. You'll learn how to obtain the all-important law-enforcement report, fill out an identity-theft affidavit, and then create your successful plan of attack.

You Think You're a Victim

In This Chapter

- ◆ Identity theft is common and easy
- ◆ How identity theft works
- ◆ Confirming the identity theft
- ◆ Your rights can help you fight the fraud

Perhaps bills came in with purchases you didn't recognize. A credit-card company called, claiming you owe $20,000—but you didn't have an account with the company. Your bank statement showed checks cashed out of your account, but when you reviewed the checks themselves, the name and address on the checks were not yours. Maybe you're a licensed contractor who's been receiving letters from lawyers demanding that you make good on work you don't remember doing. Or maybe you were stopped for speeding, only to be arrested for an outstanding warrant for a crime you never committed.

You're not in the middle of a secret reality show or a bad made-for-television movie. No, the problem—and maybe the reason you are reading this book—is that someone stole your identity. And this book is going to help you set everything right and reclaim your good name.

What Is Identity Theft?

If this has already happened to you, you've got a lot of company. *Identity theft* has become an enormous problem in the United States. According to law-enforcement agencies, it's the fastest-growing type of crime in this country. The Federal Trade Commission estimates that over 9 million people each year fall victim to various types of identity theft.

> **Legal Lingo**
>
> **Identity theft** is the unauthorized use of your personal identifiers for an illegal purpose. Usually the impostor steals your identity for a profit, a benefit, or possibly revenge.

Many different crimes may take place under the umbrella of identity theft. Here are just a few examples:

◆ Falsely charging purchases to someone else's credit or stealing money by debit card or check.

◆ Opening utilities in another's name.

◆ Posing as someone else to receive medical treatment at no cost.

◆ Getting an apartment or mortgage in someone else's name without his or her knowledge.

> **Information = Power**
>
> Individuals are not the sole victims of identity theft. Some thieves pretend to be businesses, leaving the real owners and entities with costs, reputation ruin, and angry customers and suppliers.

Chances are that you'll never learn who did this, nor how. All it took was an unscrupulous fraudster getting some of your personal information, probably through exploiting the good and trusting nature of people, businesses, and even government agencies.

Some crooks will buy the information from other criminals. Others might go into dumpsters and trash bins—nicknamed "dumpster-diving" by law-enforcement—looking for account statements that have credit numbers or Social Security numbers on them. There are fraudsters who work at a business and will steal credit-card numbers, expiration dates, and sensitive, personal data, racking up purchases in their off hours. Here are some examples of personal information that are often easy to steal or find and that can help a criminal take on your identity:

- Name
- Driver's license number
- Social Security number
- Bank account number, checking account number, investment/ retirement account numbers
- Credit/debit card numbers
- Home address
- Place of employment
- Mother's maiden name
- Description of physical appearance
- Passport number
- Health/dental insurance number
- Professional license number

Hidden Agenda

An identity thief may not need more than one or two pieces of your personal information to cause trouble. In a criminal practice called synthetic identity theft, the fraudster might take your Social Security number, another person's name, an address to receive credit cards, and put them together to create a fake identity. Because this country uses Social Security numbers as a de facto national ID, eventually creditors and sometimes law enforcement go after the person whose Social Security number was used.

Even though committing identity theft can be easy, cleaning up the mess is a challenge.

What Happens When Your Identity Is Stolen

Fraudsters who steal your identity aren't doing so for the pleasure of pretending to be you. They usually are doing it for financial gain, avoiding arrest or prosecution, or for revenge. An identity thief uses your personal information as a way to "prove" to some company or institution that he or she is actually you to obtain financial benefits, hurt your reputation, or protect themselves.

The whole fraud scheme is facilitated by companies and entities that do not verify or authenticate you before providing benefits or services, or before accusing you for your impostor's actions. Many organizations assume that anyone providing what they consider sufficient data about an individual must be that person!

Information = Power

As an experiment, try calling your bank or utility company to ask a question about your account. Say that you don't have your account number handy and see how much information you need to provide before the company is satisfied that you are who you say you are. Or think about how easy it is for you to place a merchandise order by phone or online and have the product sent to another address.

From the view of the organization, the crook is actually you, and they're now ready to do business with your "clone." That could mean opening a revolving charge account at a department store, opening a bank account, renting an apartment, or even getting the Post Office to forward your mail—including bills, credit card statements, and other key financial information—to another address, where the fraudster can open it and get even more personal information.

Of course, thieves aren't going to all this length to honorably undertake obligations. Instead, they will incur bills that can easily run into the tens of thousands of dollars, and far more, never pay a dime. They may pay bills for a while using convenience checks from fraudulent credit accounts in your name, keeping it up until the account goes to collections and no one will extend more credit. Then they disappear. When the bills go unpaid, the companies and institutions involved will come after you.

When I was a victim of identity theft, the woman who stole my good name used my identity for 10 months. Even after she was arrested and out on bail, she continued to apply for credit using my name and Social Security number. At the time, I met a police detective who himself was an identity-theft victim and who spent at least a year dealing with the consequences. Clearly this can happen to anyone.

The fallout from identity theft lasts months at least and can linger for years when it involves such issues as criminal identity theft or medical fraud. The consequences can go far beyond simple damage to your credit. One client of mine was not allowed to renew her driver's license because her medical record stated that she had epilepsy. A fraudster with seizures had used her identity to get medical treatment and credit.

Many identity thieves have held jobs under stolen Social Security numbers, leaving the Internal Revenue Service looking to the victims for unpaid taxes. One man contacted me who was contacted by the IRS for his fraudster's earnings for the past 15 years in another state. Some people have been arrested or convicted when thieves who stole their identities passed *themselves* off as the victims. One client of mine was actually tried for the crimes committed by her impostor. Another client couldn't get a job because the impostor had a felony record.

If all that isn't bad enough, the emotional ride you take as a victim is devastating. You've been violated: first by the impostor, then by the fact that corporate or law-enforcement entities don't believe you. You'll feel angry and frustrated as people call or write, accusing you of one thing after another. You'll be enraged because you're considered guilty until you're proven innocent.

 Identity Crisis

One of the worst things is that, even though identity theft is so common, many people will assume that you're simply making excuses for what you (your impostor) did. In the land of presumption of innocence, you are presumed guilty and will have to prove that you have done nothing wrong. This is perhaps the ultimate case of blaming the victim.

But let's not get off-track. It's upsetting, it's painful, but it's not an incurable disease. By using this book and letting me help you, you can and will get your identity back and return to a normal life—and, most importantly, restore your good name and be far wiser as a result. The first step is determining whether you are the victim of identity theft or just a victim of a mixed-up file or other bureaucratic error.

How to Confirm the Theft

Unfortunately, there is no iron-clad test of whether someone stole your identity. However, there are indicators—signs that someone is pretending to be you. Here are just a few you may experience:

- ◆ You start getting bills for financial obligations you didn't take on.

- ◆ You stop getting bills, credit card statements, bank statements, and other documents at your billing address, with no explanation.

- ◆ Companies deny you credit or give you unfavorable terms, even though you thought you had stellar credit.

- ◆ Collection agencies start writing and calling about accounts you don't have.

- ◆ Police arrest you for some offense you didn't commit.

- ◆ Your application for health insurance is denied because of a pre-existing condition you don't have.

- ◆ You are not eligible for worker's compensation because someone using your name and Social Security number is already receiving it.

However, if you have a suspicion of fraud, there's a good chance that someone has stolen your identity. You need to move fast to confirm that identity theft has taken place, so that, if it has, you can immediately start to set things right.

First, check your credit reports. Chapter 4 covers in detail how to get and understand your credit report, as well as what to do should you find that you're an identity-theft victim and how to clean up the problems.

Hidden Agenda _____

It can be easy to confuse honest mistakes with identity theft. For example, I know someone who suddenly had his electric utility account cancelled without notice. Although that could have been a sign of identity theft, what happened was a family moving a few houses down mistakenly gave his street number when setting up bills and forwarding their mail. The electric company assumed that he must have moved out of his house. If you have a common name like Smith or Jones, your credit file may be incorrectly merged with another person with a similar name so that accounts you don't recognize appear on your credit profile.

Go over all of your financial statements—from banks, insurance companies, credit-card companies, retirement accounts, and any businesses that have issued you credit—and look for any activity that appears unauthorized.

For any collection agency that contacts you, send in writing via U.S. mail (return receipt requested) that you dispute the charges as fraud and that you demand that they stop collections and request to immediately see all paperwork and records backing their claims.

If there is activity that isn't yours, telephone the organization and see if there might have been an honest mistake. If not, then, sorry to say, you're an identity-theft victim. But, again, take heart. You will get through this and come out on the other side.

Your Rights as a Victim

As a victim of identity theft, it's vital to remember that you have rights, for two reasons. First, having steps that you are legally entitled to take that can improve and eventually right the situation will be a real comfort for most victims of financial fraud. Believe me, I know. When I was victimized in 1996, there were no laws that protected identity-theft victims. I had to discover how to fix my own problem. Afterward, I got involved and even helped write and testify for the laws that protect you today. You may feel like you're lost in the woods, uncertain of where you are, but this book will be like a map and compass to guide you to safety.

The second reason is that you may find that the staff at collection agencies, creditors, banks—even some law-enforcement agencies—don't know the law or your rights. Understanding your rights is the best way to educate those who can help you to get what you need and deserve. What follows is a summary of those rights. The rest of the book is about how to put them into action for you.

Your Rights and Credit

The major tool you have under federal law is the Fair Credit Reporting Act (FCRA), which was amended by the Fair and Accurate Credit Transactions Act (FACTA) in 2003, which really addressed identity theft for the first time. Here's what it guarantees you, both in terms of creditors and credit-reporting agencies (CRAs):

◆ By phone you can place a fraud alert on your CRA credit files for 90 days. You can make a written request to extend a fraud alert for up to seven years.

◆ You have the right to two free credit reports in the year after you file an extended alert, and the credit bureaus must provide you your file not more than three business days after your request. All consumers are entitled to an annual free disclosure of your consumer report from each of the three credit-reporting companies and other specialty consumer reporting agencies. The specialty consumer reporting agencies provide a range of information on people, including check-writing history, employment history, insurance claims, medical history, and tenant history.

◆ For five years from the date you write and request an extended alert, the consumer credit-reporting agencies must exclude you from any consumer lists it prepares and gives to any third party to offer pre-screened credit or insurance; you can opt out of unsolicited credit and insurance offers based on CRA-provided information by calling 1-888-5-OPT-OUT (more details in Chapter 4).

◆ You can dispute fraudulent information in your credit report and the CRAs must block fraudulent information from displaying in your credit report, once you identify that information as fraud by providing an identity-theft report. The data cannot be reinserted in your file unless the creditor verifies to the CRA that the information was indeed correct.

♦ Any business or agency that created a fraudulent account for an identity thief is required to give you all documentation about transactions that the thief undertook and provide it to your law-enforcement agency within 30 days at no cost.

♦ Collection agencies must stop their collection activity when you tell them that a debt is fraudulent, notify the original creditor, and send you (on request) all information about the debt so you can dispute it.

♦ A creditor may not sell a debt to collections after it is notified that the debit was due to fraud. If a collection company is notified by a victim that a debt is fraudulent, the collection company must stop collections, notify the original creditor, and, upon request of the victim, provide all information about the debt in order to dispute it.

> **Legal Lingo**
>
> A **credit-reporting agency** (CRA) is a company that collects credit information on consumers and sells that information, in the form of credit reports, to other companies, landlords, lenders, potential employers, and others. The three main CRAs are Trans Union, Experian, and Equifax.

I'll cover how to use these rights and others for you in reclaiming and restoring your identity throughout the rest of this book.

Your Rights and Law Enforcement

Under the FCRA, you will need to present an identity-theft report from any law-enforcement agency. Given federal statutes and the laws of most states, identity theft is a crime and you have a right to ask any local, state, or federal law-enforcement agency to file an identity-theft report on your behalf.

Unfortunately, some local agencies are reluctant to issue an identity-theft report, because they don't have the resources to investigate. The FBI or Secret Service, who have jurisdiction for these crimes, will not investigate unless there are dozens of victims from a particular impostor (in other words, a large security breach) or unless there is a very high dollar value. So those agencies may send you to local law-enforcement agencies, which may be understaffed, overwhelmed with cases, or not willing to see you as a victim, since often the credit-card companies are still considered the real victims. Your local postal inspector or Social Security inspector, as federal agents, have the authority to give you an identity-theft report, but often are so busy that they will refer you to local police. You may also ask for a report from your Department of Motor Vehicles.

Federal law, as do most state penal codes, entitles you to be recognized as a victim (18 USC 1028), and you must have an identity-theft report to clear your name, so don't give up if an agency refuses to give you one. Call the managing officer of the agency. If all else fails, call the Federal Trade Commission at 1-877-ID-THEFT to ask for assistance.

No matter what, you have the right to politely ask for an *informational* report that will include your documentation of the fraudulent activity and phony addresses. You have this right because identity fraud is a crime under both federal and state law. (See the next section for more on state laws.) There may be multiple federal law-enforcement agencies you can contact as well. Chapter 3 has detailed help on how to file reports with law enforcement.

You also have rights if the identity thief used your name or Social Security number when arrested, creating a criminal record under your name:

- ◆ You have a right to your own copy of the (fraudulent) criminal record in your name, including the booking records, court documents, and state and federal database records from the courts and from the National Crime Information Center (NCIC).

- ◆ You can file an impersonation report and identity-theft report.

- ◆ You can have the police confirm your identity and help you prove that you are not the impersonator. You can request that the law-enforcement agency issue you a clearance letter.

- ◆ You can ask the appropriate district attorney to amend any complaint against you and have the law-enforcement agency correct all its records.

- ◆ You have the right to have the courts correct all their records.

- ◆ You have the right to correct background checks showing the arrests/convictions with consumer reporting agencies.

Chapter 15 covers all this in detail.

Other Federal Identity Theft and Privacy Laws

A number of laws also provide you certain rights as a victim of identity theft. The Fair Credit Reporting Act (FCRA, 15 USC §§1681 to 1681u) regulates consumer reports and consumer-reporting agencies. Section 5 of the Fair and Accurate Credit Transactions Act (FACTA), an amendment to the FCRA, specifically addresses identity theft and related consumer issues. Victims of identity theft are granted the ability to work with creditors and credit bureaus to remove negative information in their credit report resulting from identity theft. FACTA also enables consumers to place three different types of fraud alerts intended to stop credit grantors from opening any new accounts.

The Gramm-Leach-Bliley Act (GLBA), also known as the Financial Services Modernization Act of 1999, provides limited privacy protections against the sale of consumer financial information, including "Fraudulent Access to Financial Information."

The Truth in Lending Act limits liability for fraudulent credit card charges to $50.00, in most situations. It also requires "meaningful disclosure" of key information in any consumer-credit transaction.

The Fair Credit Billing Act establishes procedures for resolving billing errors or fraud on credit-card accounts when the consumer reports such unauthorized activity within certain time frames.

The Electronic Fund Transfer Act provides a basic framework of the rights, liabilities, and responsibilities of parties involved in making electronic fund transfers. It grants identity-theft rights when using electronic transfers including debit cards for financial transactions.

The Health Insurance Portability and Accountability Act of 1996 (HIPAA) requires healthcare providers and insurers to create and maintain electronic patient records, in order to improve confidentiality and efficiency. A patient has certain privacy rights; however, a provider does not need consent to disclose patient information for situations involving treatment, payment, and healthcare operations. HIPAA also mandates a duty to disclose security breaches to affected individuals. It also allows patients to dispute errors like identity fraud. See Fact Sheet 8a regarding HIPAA at www.privacyrights.org.

In the United States, privacy and identity-theft issues are also within the jurisdiction of the states. Your state of residence may have laws that grant you additional rights.

Contact your state's Attorney General's office and ask about identity-theft victim's rights. For contact information, check with the National Association of Attorneys General (www.naag.org). There is a map on the home page with links to contact information for each state's AG.

The site LLRX.com has a good collection of state identity-theft victim resources. Go to www.llrx.com and search for identity-theft rights. Also see the National Conference of State Legislators at www.ncls.org and search for identity theft.

The Least You Need to Know

◆ Identity theft may manifest in ways other than credit. Anything you can do with your identity can be done by impostors.

◆ It is easy for thieves to get enough personal information about you to pretend to be you. No one is immune.

◆ You must take steps to verify whether you are an identity-theft victim, and then prove your innocence.

◆ You have some powerful legal rights as a victim that will help you clear your name.

Chapter 2

First Things First

In This Chapter

- What you're up against
- Organizing for success
- Communicating effectively

You wouldn't dream of going on a cross-country automobile trip without getting your car checked. Before serving a Thanksgiving dinner for more extended family than you remembered you had, you put hours into chopping vegetables and baking pies. Regaining your identity is no different. You have to prepare, and that process starts here.

What You're Facing—But Don't Panic

This isn't going to be fun or easy, but you will learn a great deal about protecting yourself. You're far better off knowing what you need for the venture ahead so you can be ready and make it as painless as possible. The only other option is to do nothing, in which case your experience will only be worse.

Information = Power

In his famous comic science fiction novel, *The Hitchhiker's Guide to the Galaxy,* author Douglas Adams offered a bit of fundamental advice: Don't Panic. That needs to become your mantra throughout this process. Even when things get tough, there's a way through them.

Complex and Time-Consuming

Identity recovery is a challenging process that will eat up many hours of your time. You start by getting records from a few sources. The information you get will send you to even more sources. At each step of the way, you have to keep track of and document everything.

The whole process is repetitive and nonlinear. You don't just go from step A to B to C. You'll go from A to B, then out to G, back to C, over to F, back to A, and so on. You'll get one financial record, talk to someone about that, find out another detail, go off in a different direction, come back to the first records, and continue untangling the damage done to you. But you'll be empowered by what you learn.

This is time consuming, and the course of recovery can require many hours of time over a period of months. In particularly bad cases like criminal identity theft, getting your identity back can literally take years. But you can't let up, because if you do, you can lose important legal rights.

As you work through the process, you'll often find situations and tasks that demand attention and that can be distracting. However, it doesn't have to become your whole life. Remember, 100 hours spread over 10 months is just 10 hours a month. You may need to take a few days off work to get this done, though. Larger blocks of time allow for more effective telephone follow-up, which is best accomplished during working hours.

Expenses

The process of recovering your identity may involve some expenses, including any or all of the following:

- Photocopying costs to get copies of your various records

- Postage and shipping

- Long-distance telephone charges

- Car mileage

- Tape recording media and transcription

- Court transcripts

- Lawyer fees

Hidden Agenda _____

There is a mythical story of Alexander the Great and the Gordian Knot. An oracle foretold that the man who could undo a fabled incredibly tangled knot would rule the known world. Many had unsuccessfully tried their hand. Alexander came up, sliced through the knot with his sword, and went on to add "the Great" to his name. Unfortunately, no blade will cut through your identity complications. But, like straightening a snarled cord, you will succeed.

Don't get prematurely upset. For most financial fraud (which is the majority of identity theft), you won't need a lawyer and court transcripts won't be an issue. But such expenses are common enough in identity-recovery cases, and you're better off preparing for the worst. Then you can at least be pleasantly surprised if the cost is lower.

Hidden Agenda _____

According to an Identity Theft Resource Survey of 2008 identity-theft victims, the average cost in out-of-pocket expenses was $739 for damage done to existing credit or financial accounts. When the fraudster created one or more new accounts, the average cost to the victim was $951.

Most important to remember: The financial, professional, physical, emotional, and mental cost, as well as the damage to your personal reputation, of leaving your identity theft unchecked will far outstrip any time you'll spend fixing it.

Potential Confrontations

Many people find confrontation extremely difficult. Either they run from it, giving way to whatever someone else wants, or they jump in swinging, eager to get any fight over with. Neither of these choices is useful; you need to *gently* confront. Be politely assertive, organized, and prepared with your information when dealing with companies and governmental entities. That will help you get the cooperation necessary to recovering your identity.

Information = Power

The strong reaction you may have toward confrontation can come from the classic, animal fight-or-flight response that humans still carry, or it can be conditioning from your environment, upbringing, and personal nature. The more you understand why you react a certain way, the greater your chances of objectively dealing with your emotions and resolving your identity-theft issues.

Instead of reacting, you must take control and understand where you might find confrontation and what its origins likely are. Your run-ins will most likely be with the very people from whom you need information or help, including law enforcement, financial-services companies, credit bureaus, creditors, collection bureaus, health-care providers, and so many others. They are the people you'll be in contact with most often. Many of them don't know how to help you, or they may be over-whelmed themselves, but stay calm. If you lose your cool, you will be reacting to any of a number of conditions:

- The people don't know what the law requires.

- Their organizations instruct them to act a certain way, possibly including not providing you information.

- Your requests will throw off their busy schedules and they have to deal with the disruptive results, not you.

- You've caught them on a bad day, and fraud departments are over-worked and understaffed.

- They think there is a chance that you're using identity theft as an excuse to get away with something.

◆ What you perceive is actually your own anxiety and impatience projected onto them.

◆ They are frustrated themselves.

Identity Crisis _____

It's possible that, during the process of investigating your fraud, you might come in contact with the thief who put you into this situation. Resist the temptation to engage this person. Do not accept an opportunity to see or speak with the fraudster. The person is a criminal, is unlikely to help you, and may be dangerous. The only potential exception might be if the person is a family member or former friend. In that case, check Chapter 11 for specific advice.

Telling yourself not to have a particular emotional response is useless, because you cannot wish your feelings away. What you can do is develop an intellectual response to keep things in check. Here are a few thoughts to help you keep control.

Before you call an agency or company, remind yourself of what is truly important: regaining control of your identity. Write down what you plan to say, including a concise summation of background facts, and what you need. Be aware of your rights as a victim (see Chapter 1), and be ready to ask what they need from you so they may help you.

Remember that you are talking to someone who has his own life and responsibilities, as well as a job to keep. Even if you have a legal right to what you seek, you are also asking this person for a favor. Manners go a long way in helping you succeed. If possible, put yourself in the shoes of the other person, empathize with them, and be interested in them. Not only does it help dispel a negative reaction, it increases the chance that they might willingly go out of their way for you.

Also remember that the person you're speaking to was not responsible for the identity theft. Don't unfairly blame him or her and take out on them the anger you feel toward the thief or entity that facilitated the fraud. At the very least, be polite, even when you must firmly insist on obtaining the information you need to which you have a legal right.

Again, this approach is to keep your emotions from getting the better of you. Still, at times you may find yourself getting frustrated and over-whelmed. It's a natural reaction, but don't give in. Stay focused. Don't waste lots of time with someone who has no authority. If they can't help you, ask for the name and phone number of someone who can. Ask to speak with a supervisor who may have the ability to help you.

Get Organized

In terms of preparation, getting organized is the single most important thing you can do. Proper organization offers a host of benefits that will be critical to your success:

- ◆ You appear more professional, and the companies, organizations, agencies, and personnel with whom you deal will take you more seriously and be more responsive.

- ◆ Being organized will increase your confidence, making you more effective and reducing the stress and anxiety of the process.

- ◆ Having all the results of your inquiries and investigations at your fingertips will help you prove violations of the law *and* your inno-cence, both of which are necessary to make the changes you need to your records, as well as to get help from a lawyer, if things come to that.

- ◆ When you have all your losses and expenses organized, you may be able to deduct them from your taxes under 165e of the U.S. tax code, saving you money. In addition, if the fraudster is caught, you can prove your out-of-pocket costs and ask for restitution.

To get organized, though, you'll need to have the right approach and take a number of necessary steps.

The Right Approach

The systematic method that I'm providing you in this book will keep you from trying to reinvent the wheel. You need to approach the task of identity recovery in the most methodical way.

Put aside some time every day to get things done. There might be a given part of the day that will regularly work best, or your schedule may require you to pick different times on different days. You'll need to make phone calls during the work week and work hours, so you may need to take an early or late lunch or schedule strategic breaks, if possible. Try to complete one entire task in each sitting, whether calling or writing someone for information, reading and understanding a document, or filing a report or request for information from some organization.

Information = Power

If you study time management, you learn an important principle: it's far better to do a little bit every day than to try accomplishing everything at once. Making even one phone call or writing and sending one letter is an accomplishment and gets you closer to your goal. What seems like an overwhelming task becomes manageable when you break it into many small tasks spread out over time.

Seven Steps to Basic Organization

There are seven main steps you'll need to take to get organized:

1. Get the supplies you will need, including file folders, storage boxes, or filing cabinets (separate from your other records, so the two don't get mixed); labels, notebooks, phone logs, pens, and paper punches; a computer and printer; blank CDs or back-up drive for document backup; and a copier, scanner, and fax machine (or a combination device that does all three).

2. Create a phone log before you contact anyone. Record the following: name, with correct spelling and title; direct phone number; fax number; e-mail address; surface mail address; and date and time of the phone call.

3. Establish a filing system for paper documents. The documents go into folders labeled by category that, in turn, go into locking file drawers or storage boxes placed in locked closets. Some people might prefer using three-ring binders and loose-leaf paper. Others will want legal pads and file cabinets. Find a system that works for you.

4. For electronic documents, you want to virtually replicate your paper-filing approach. Create a folder for every file drawer or storage box. Within that folder, create others corresponding to every paper folder you have. Be sure you label them the same way and use encryption software for sensitive data, so it will be unreadable by anyone but you.

5. You want both electronic and paper versions of all documents. You will print paper versions of all electronic documents and scan all paper documents to create electronic versions. Now you see why your electronic filing system is the same as the paper one: the electronic and paper copies of a document go respectively into the electronic and paper versions of the same folder.

6. As often as you process and file documents (no more than once a day), you will copy all of your electronic files onto a back-up hard drive or recording media like CDs

Information = Power

Having a friend or family member help can make the process of recovering your identity easier. However, you will be exposing sensitive, personal data, so be careful in your choice of help.

7. If the amount of organizing seems overwhelming, recruit family members and friends to help you. Once you're set up, you'll be filling out log books and filing documents as you go, so the ongoing work becomes easily manageable.

Create Your Master Log Book

You need to track every important detail of every step of the recovery process. That's why you need a master log file for recording all information as it comes into your hands. Here's what you should put into it:

◆ Date/time sent or received

◆ Company/agency involved

◆ Name, phone number, and e-mail of contact

◆ How contact was made (phone, fax, e-mail, or letter)

- Expenses you incurred as a result (including out-of-pocket costs, time off from work, postage, fees paid to professionals, etc. It is important to log these for future tax deductions and to determine damages in a possible lawsuit.)

- Date/time that you gave/received a response

- Date/time for the next contact

- A summary of the conversation or letter

Build Your Victim Chronology

In addition to the log book, you want a running history of every step of the recovery process. Every event becomes a brief entry with a summary of that event as well as the date, time (if applicable), and a reference to any involved document so you can find it when necessary.

The chronology begins with the first indications that you might be the victim of identity theft and continues with each step as you continue your investigations. This is a critical document that shows your time and efforts. It will be helpful should you need to hire an attorney, if you must refresh your memory should to testify in court, if you are seeking restitution from a judge, or if you are settling a case with companies that may have violated the law.

Information = Power

You may not have clear details of the early stages in learning that you were a victim of identity theft because at the time you weren't thinking about rigorously pursuing recovery. Don't worry about it. Just record what you do know, referring to any records you might have that can add detail. You'll have more than enough opportunity to catch all the details going forward.

How to Handle Communications

The last area of preparation is how you are going to treat communications. You will record every communication, whether written or verbal, in the master log as well as the victim chronology from the previous section of this chapter. You also need to handle letters and telephone calls in some specific ways.

Letters

You'll be sending many letters while recovering your identity. Every time you do, in addition to making paper and electronic copies to file, be sure to send by U.S. Mail, return receipt requested. A person at the company or agency must sign a postal card to receive the letter. The Postal Service mails the card back to you as proof that the company or agency received the letter. Treat the return receipt as you would any letter, scanning a copy, filing both with the copy of the letter you sent, and making entries in the master log and victim chronology.

Identity Crisis

Having proof of delivery of letters is critical. I have literally seen companies deny that they received letters from victims until the victims sent the signed receipt. Unfortunately, large organizations often lose mail or just don't keep track of correspondence. It's sad, but true.

Phone Calls

The problem with a telephone call is that any dispute about the substance of it can too easily become a "he said, she said" issue. So after a phone conversation, which you will note in the master log and victim chronology, you send a follow-up letter (return receipt requested) giving a summary of the conversation and your understanding of what each party is to do as a result of the conversation. In your master log, record the conversation as well as when you sent the letter follow-up. If possible, you may be able to save time if you immediately send an e-mail, setting the request for receipt.

Keep copies of e-mails of receipts and document the e-mail in your master log and victim chronology. However, be aware that not all e-mail systems will send receipts, and even if they do, the e-mail could still be placed into a spam filter.

Faxes

Fax machines keep logs of when they send and receive faxes. Every time you do either, you want to print out the log record for that fax and file it, along with a copy of the fax, in your files, as well as entering the fax in the master log and victim chronology.

The Least You Need to Know

- ◆ Identity recovery involves significant challenges that you will overcome.

- ◆ Focus on what you want to achieve and be polite with people to increase the effectiveness of your efforts.

- ◆ Organization is key to success and retaining your sanity.

- ◆ Ensure that you have proof that your conversations took place and that your communications were received.

3

Your Recovery Strategy

In This Chapter

- ◆ Using investigative research to prove your innocence
- ◆ Developing a battle plan to address the identity theft and how it happened
- ◆ Leveraging law-enforcement to help clear your name

In Chapter 2, you learned what you were facing and saw how to get organized and handle communications. Now you'll start putting all this to use, because you're entering the critical investigative phase. You'll begin to pull together the documentation that shows you what happened, and then find the evidence of theft and take action.

Get the Documentation

Every step of identity recovery uses documentation, the fundamental source of the information that will help you recover your identity. As I mentioned in Chapter 2, one important source of information will be talking to people and documenting the conversations in letters and your log, but the most important resources will be the records that organizations keep. The written information will help you in a number of ways:

- Proving that you were the victim of identity theft

- Tracking down how the identity theft occurred

- Finding additional sources to help you recover your identity

- Showing how an organization may be financially responsible for the results of the identity theft

I'm going to give you an overview of the records that you'll need most in recovering your identity. Other chapters will tell you how to get and interpret them. I'm going to break this information down into two categories: financial and other.

Identity Crisis

These records are necessary, but may not show the full extent of the documentation you'll eventually need if the fraudster has created new credit accounts, utility accounts, apartment leases, bank accounts, or other fraud in your name. Later in this chapter, I explain how to create a plan of attack to deal with such problems.

Financial

The financial industry keeps extensive records, so you can get the details that will help you investigate your case of stolen identity. About 80 percent of identity theft is financial in nature, so records from financial institutions will be the most important documents for investigating and resolving your case of identity theft.

- Credit reports

- Credit-card statements

- Bank statements

- Investment accounts

- Insurance policies and accounts

- Service accounts

Credit reports are documents kept by CRAs that will likely become the most powerful tool you have to investigate your identity theft. They show who inquires about your credit record, which entities have granted credit in your name, and which organizations are reporting problems getting credit payments from you. Chapter 4 covers credit reports and how to work with them in detail.

Information = Power

If you stop getting any regular financial statements, including those from credit-card companies, your bank, cell-phone service providers, or utility companies, it's a strong indication that someone might have stolen your identity and changed the address that the company has for you.

Your monthly credit-card statements show what was charged, when it was charged, and what organizations placed the charges when the thief used your credit-card number. Chapter 5 covers how to handle credit-card problems.

Your monthly bank or financial institution statements offer the best indicator of whether someone has committed check fraud, debit-card fraud, fraudulent wire transfers, or some other fraudulent activity. You'll know because debit memos will be listed on the statements. Chapter 7 has the details on how to get them. Statements from investment accounts will show if someone has sold some or all of your portfolio and taken the money. Look at Chapter 7 for more details.

You'll also want any documents relating to insurance policies and accounts. A criminal could try to cash out certain types of life insurance policies, file a fraudulent claim on a policy, or change the coverage of a policy in anticipation of a fraudulent claim. Chapter 8 tells you how to get the records. Health insurance is in the category of medical records, which I mention later in this chapter.

Also check records from service accounts such as cell-phone providers and utilities, which regularly bill you for service, to see if account information has changed or if there are unexplained charges. Chapter 8 has information on these.

Other Records

This category is a grab-bag because of the variety of records that might be important. Look through all of them to see what could apply.

◆ **Social Security PEBES:** Getting your *personal earnings and benefit estimate statement* from the Social Security Administration can alert you if the thief is using your Social Security number at a job and potentially leaving the Internal Revenue Service bill for you. Go to Chapter 12 for details.

> **Legal Lingo** _____
>
> A **personal earnings and benefit estimate statement (PEBES)** is a form that the Social Security Administration sends you to show the history of earnings it has on record for you by year and an estimate of the resulting future Social Security benefits. Any earnings that you don't recognize may be the work of an impersonator.

◆ **Criminal identity theft and background checks:** Identity thieves are often involved in other sorts of illegal activity, which can create law-enforcement havoc. Some fraudsters, when arrested in another crime, will give your name to keep charges from going on their own records. You'll need to do a background check on yourself to ensure that you haven't been made the target of law enforcement. The details of how to get a background check and how to handle criminal identity theft in Chapter 15.

◆ **Public records checks:** These records show you what public records are associated with your name, including lawsuits, birth records, and licenses.

◆ **Online records:** Cyber identity theft is one of the fastest-growing areas because it gives crooks more ways to take other parts of your personal identity, or even the identity of your business. Online records could include social-networking accounts, accounts with Internet service providers, and websites that mention you or your business. Because there can be so many sources of information to check, you should look at Chapter 17 for some details of how to proceed.

◆ **Medical records:** Medical identity theft, like criminal identity theft, is a category largely unto itself, because there aren't established steps to remedy the problem in the same way as with financial identity theft. If you have any indication that your medical identity has been stolen, like getting bills or collection calls for medical procedures you never had, you'll want to check health insurance and medical records. Chapter 14 explains how.

Create a Plan of Attack

Now that you have documents to show what has been happening, you can determine the size of the problem and then create your plan to stop the fraud and restore your good name.

Understand the Scope

Congratulations, you are about to take on a new job as a combination private investigator and detective as you sort out what has happened. Here are the initial steps to take:

1. Read through every report, letter, or document and circle items that you were not responsible for.

2. Make phone calls to the organization to find out what you can, and get valid addresses to send fraud-dispute letters.

3. Enter this information into your victim chronology and master log. (See Chapter 2 for information on creating these.)

4. Create a list of tasks for each problem, such as who to call, who to write, what to write, and what information to gather.

A critical aspect of understanding the scope of the identity theft is knowing what aspects of your identity the thief has compromised.

◆ Credit items appearing on your credit reports

◆ Other financial concerns like banking accounts, securities, and utility accounts that don't appear on credit reports

◆ Legal issues (including criminal charges and lawsuits)

- Government identity challenges (including any government-issued identification as well as state-issued professional licenses)

- Insurance matters (like use of auto, health, or life insurance in your name)

- Special cases, including medical and cyber identity theft, theft of a minor's identity, identity theft perpetrated by a relative or friend, or workplace-related identity theft

Information = Power

Always check for credit bureau and government identity issues, even if you're a victim of criminal identity theft or employment fraud and you don't suspect a credit problem. If you're the victim of any identity theft, your fraudster probably wants your credit, too. A credit report is also the single most useful tool for uncovering most financial identity theft. And you always need to take some action regarding the postal service because the fraudster will change your address and use the mail to obtain fraudulent accounts, loans, credit cards, or other benefits.

Different aspects will require different tactics to correct. Now that you've got a list of what parts of your identity may be affected, look at the appropriate following sections for the steps you'll need to take and the chapters in the book that will tell you what to do.

Creditors

No matter what type of identity theft you think is happening, always look at the records that the CRAs keep. Credit records can provide early warning signs you won't find any other way. Chapter 4 details how to get your credit report, what information you might find, what you can learn from the report, and how to clean the record.

If collection agencies are contacting you, if there are collection accounts or liens in your credit report, or if you see inquiries from companies you don't know accessing your credit profile, Chapter 4 also shows you how to deal with them.

If you find problems with fraud on your own credit-card accounts, such as MasterCard, Visa, American Express, and Discover, read Chapter 5 for details on what to do. (Note that business credit-card accounts are different and I cover them later in this chapter.)

For any other accounts or inquiries listed on the credit report, including new-account fraud, such as loans, department-store accounts, medical-collection accounts, and IRS liens, see Chapter 6. For more information on medical fraud or if any healthcare provider has made a report on your credit report, see Chapter 14.

Financial Institutions

There is financial identity theft that doesn't appear on credit reports. This will include bank fraud (including debit cards, checks, money orders, cashier's checks, and wire transfers), and securities fraud of investment accounts (including pensions, 401(k)s, stocks, mutual funds, and *Health Savings Accounts*). See Chapter 7 for details on how to deal with all of these.

There are other types of financial identity theft and fraud that don't appear on your credit profile:

- Cell phones and phone cards

- Apartment leases

- Utilities

- Certain types of credit cards, like gasoline cards

Chapter 8 has the details of how to deal with all of these.

Legal Lingo

Health Savings Accounts (HSAs) are special savings accounts available to persons who enroll in high-deductible health-insurance plans. The HSA savings are supposed to pay for the high deductibles unpaid by the carrier. These savings plans are set up with pre tax dollars and when the funds are used to pay qualifying uncovered medical expenses, those monies are not taxable.

Legal Issues

Although not the most common problem for identity-theft victims, when there are legal issues the results can be some of the most expensive, disruptive, and upsetting possible. A fraudster placed under arrest or charged with criminal activity may have given your identity to authorities or otherwise left you looking like the guilty party. If you learned that your impostor had criminal arrests or convictions, go to Chapter 15 to learn how to deal with those issues.

You may also face personal injury, breach of contract, and other civil lawsuits or even liens by the IRS for actions the thief has taken. In that case, Chapter 16 has the relevant details of what to do.

Government Agencies

You may find that you have to deal with various government agencies. This could involve any of the following:

◆ IRS liens (Chapters 6, 12, and 16)

◆ Worker's compensation, veteran's benefits, child support, or alimony (Chapter 12)

◆ Government-issued IDs or security clearances (Chapter 12)

◆ Professional licenses (Chapter 12)

Insurance Companies

Insurance fraud, including car, life, disability, and health, is dealt with in Chapter 8. In addition, problems with health insurance are strong indicators of medical identity theft. In that case, you also need to read Chapter 14.

Special Cases

Certain types of identity theft require a different approach to getting information and fixing the problem. For each type, I've devoted a separate chapter (though you will need the information in other relevant chapters as well):

◆ Medical identity theft (Chapter 14)

◆ Identity theft of your child (Chapter 9)

◆ Identity theft of someone who died (Chapter 10)

◆ Identity theft by a family member or friend (Chapter 11)

◆ Workplace identity theft, which can include business credit cards (Chapter 13)

◆ Online or cyber identity theft (Chapter 17)

Creating the Criminal Paper Trail

A person who steals your identity is breaking the law and is a criminal. You need to treat the person as a criminal by properly reporting the fraud to law-enforcement authorities. Ignoring this step has some dire consequences:

♦ Without an identity-theft report, you lose valuable rights (including getting evidence and some types of information for free, blocking fraudulent information in a timely manner, and stopping collections) that you need to reclaim your identity.

♦ Most companies and organizations will ignore your requests because they will assume that the claims of identity theft are fictitious.

♦ You lose credibility and access to tools that can help keep the theft from spreading.

The next two steps—preparing an affidavit and getting a formal identity-theft report from an appropriate law-enforcement agency—are critical.

Identity Crisis

Even though filing a criminal report is a standard and necessary step in regaining your identity and protecting yourself from the results of identity theft, it's more complicated when the theft was committed by a family member or (former) friend. In that case, read Chapter 11, because I'll give you other tools to treat it differently if you can get the identity thief to appropriately cooperate.

FTC ID Theft Affidavit

Working with financial institutions, credit grantors, and consumer advocates, the Federal Trade Commission has developed an ID Theft Affidavit, which is accepted by most institutions in our country. You can get a copy online by going to www.ftc.gov/bcp/edu/resources/forms/affidavit.pdf or by calling 1-877-ID-THEFT (1-877-438-4338).

This model document is a single form that simplifies the process of alerting companies to your identity-theft scenario. Using this one form (and the many copies you'll likely need) will provide you with a number of benefits:

♦ Saving you time in retelling the events

♦ Providing a format that virtually all creditors, agencies, and financial institutions will accept

♦ Aiding law enforcement when you seek an *identity-theft report*

> **Legal Lingo** _____
>
> An **identity-theft report** is a document, created by a local, state, or federal law-enforcement agency, providing official notice that you are the victim of identity theft. You'll need to obtain a copy of the filed report and make copies as needed.

You can't just get your identity-theft report and think your work is over. As your investigative and recovery work progresses, you will need to update the law-enforcement report with the agency that provided the report, and you'll need to continue to update the affidavit to reflect the most current information. It is a good idea to attach your victim chronology to your affidavit if you omit confidential information that should not be seen by everyone.

You may find that some entities ask you to fill out multiple affidavits of fraud and have them notarized. Under the law, you do not need to notarize them—just provide the FTC affidavit. If a creditor is being difficult and insists on a notarized affidavit, notarize one copy of the affidavit, make copies, and then send them a copy, unless they offer to pay for you to obtain and send a separately notarized copy.

> **Information = Power** _____
>
> Your bank will provide a bank guaranty of your signature at no cost. If a creditor wants a notarized affidavit, offer a copy of the bank signature verification. If a creditor continues to demand an original, notarized affidavit, report the company to the Federal Trade Commission at 1-877-IDTHEFT. You should not have to notarize documents unless the creditor is willing to pay for the notary's fee.

Filing Law-Enforcement Reports

Filing an identity-theft report with law enforcement is critical. It proves to creditors that you've been the victim of identity theft and, when sent along with a letter, affidavit, and identifying documents to the credit bureaus, it obliges CRAs to block (temporarily delete) all fraudulent accounts listed on your credit report.

Because federal and state laws make identity theft a crime, a law-enforcement organization is obligated to take a report on a case. However, there's a difference between obligation and action. Sometimes getting a law-enforcement department to write an identity-theft report can be difficult for a number of reasons:

- The department may be overworked and understaffed and is concerned that writing the report will force it to investigate.

- Officials may view identity theft as minor compared to such crimes as assault and robbery, and not as deserving of attention.

- A law-enforcement department or agency may be concerned about driving up crime statistics

- Law-enforcement personnel may view the creditors, who lose the money, as the victims rather than you.

- Law enforcement may not understand that the FCRA requires an identity-theft report for many of your rights.

Be sure to explain to the law-enforcement agency how important this is. If you don't get the report, you will bear the economic loss, and both your financial and personal reputation are at stake. Identity theft can affect your ability to get credit, to get a job, or to buy a house or rent an apartment. It is a serious problem and you need help to deal with it.

If you find law enforcement reluctant to help, state that you want a report "for informational purposes, only." That allows them to fill out a report without legal obligation to investigate the complaint.

Some law-enforcement departments may try to insist that the creditor file a report before they can give you a report. Many creditors won't file a police report because it will be time consuming for their fraud department and they don't want to experience more economic loss. It is frustrating for law enforcement when the companies won't cooperate. To help them understand, refer to the Fair Credit Reporting Act 605B (15 U.S.C. §1681C-2), which states that an identity-theft report is needed for victims to block fraud with the credit reporting agencies. You are not trying to make their job harder; you need the report to regain your good credit.

Identity Crisis

An identity-theft report must include specific reference to the fraudulent accounts. You can make a copy of your credit report available to the department or agency, but only after you have blacked out personal identifying information like your Social Security number, real account numbers, and personal information. Police reports are public records and you don't want to make life easy for another fraudster or give up your privacy. It's better to show them the credit reports, but give a separate list of all the fraud information to attach to the report.

Because identity theft involves both state and federal laws, you often have some flexibility in where you ultimately obtain the identity-theft report. Your local or state police or even the DMV can provide a report because you, the victim, live in their jurisdiction.

If there is evidence that the fraud crosses state boundaries, if the dollar amount is very high, if there is evidence of a fraud ring, of if terrorists are involved, the local office of the FBI or of the Secret Service can investigate, especially if there are multiple victims.

If the fraudster used mail in any way to steal your identity and perpetrate fraud, U.S. Postal Service inspectors can provide an identity-theft report and may even investigate.

If the identity thief makes use of your Social Security number, then you can also ask investigators at your local Social Security Administration office for a report.

Be sure to ask if there is a cost to obtain the report (usually you have to pay for the copies). When you request the report by phone or in person, be sure to address the following:

◆ State that you do not yet know the extent to which your identity has been used.

- List any accounts or other information that you know for certain are fraudulent.

- Provide any address or other potential contact information found on your credit report for the perpetrator. (For example, if you have an address to where fraudulent credit cards were sent, provide it.)

- If there is a cost for the report, include payment with a letter of request for the report.

- Ask for updates on information if the agency is willing to investigate. You will be able to provide your own updates in writing. Ask to be allowed to add addendums to the report.

- Indicate that you understand there can be confidentiality issues, but that they do not apply to documents with your own confidential and personal information, so documents they discover with your name on them should be copied for you for evidence.

- Request that the police report include the list you provide of all the accounts that have been the subject of fraud.

- Show them a copy of your Identity-Theft Affidavit as well as a copy of a government-issued ID and a copy of a utility bill for identification purposes. Remember to blacken out any sensitive data.

Also, be sure to get the name, phone number, address, and e-mail address of the law-enforcement official who took the report. Remember that only 10 percent of cases get investigated, but if you provide lots of evidence, your case may become one of them.

The Least You Need to Know

- Your financial, credit, and public records will help you investigate the identity theft.

- A background check will show if you have become the target of law enforcement or if someone is working using your name, has purchased property, or obtained a license or other benefit with your identity.

◆ Determine which types of fraud are involved.

◆ Obtain an identity-theft report from a law-enforcement agency.

◆ Complete an Identity-Theft Affidavit and make copies to send to any entity involved with the fraud.

Part 2

Restore Your Finances

Most identity theft is financial fraud, so this part is likely to be critically important to you. Understanding how to obtain, read, and use your credit reports will become the cornerstone of your recovery effort. You'll learn how to correct various types of financial fraud committed in your name, including credit and loan accounts, as well as how to deal with relentless collection agencies. You'll discover how to rectify frauds that won't show up on your credit report, including various types of check and wire scams and investment and insurance fraud.

Chapter 4

Credit Reports

In This Chapter

- The "big stick" of identity recovery
- Reading the report
- Looking for the red flags
- Lodging the formal complaints

Throughout this book you'll find almost constant mention of CRAs and credit reports. That's because for most victims, the credit report is the foundation of investigating their financial identity theft and the cornerstone of clearing their names. Even if you think that your identity theft isn't financial in nature, read though this chapter and use what you learn, because chances are that you're going to need it.

The Mother of All Restoration Tools

Credit files and reports, as well as the CRAs that create and maintain them, are important in identity recovery for a number of reasons. Fraudulent accounts or activity on your credit report damage your reputation and keep you from freely living your life. Your credit file is a personal credit history and, as such, a fundamental part of your financial life. Anyone with a bona-fide business need is allowed to gain access to your credit report, including companies issuing you credit, landlords, potential employers, and certain government agencies. Most of the time you give permission for businesses to get your credit report when you apply for credit. Landlords and potential employers will also get your permission to access your credit profile.

Because of its central role in finance and credit, the credit report becomes one of the more effective ways of examining who is issuing credit in your name and who is reporting payment problems. It is a central information repository of all credit, collections, and liens in your name. The Fair Credit Reporting Act (see Chapter 1 for details) and many state laws give you significant rights in obtaining and challenging information in your credit report. To secure your rights under the Fair Credit Reporting Act, you must dispute credit-report records with CRAs before you dispute them with individual creditors listed on your credit report.

Identity Crisis

You *must* dispute the fraud on your credit reports with the CRAs immediately after you've received copies of the credit reports. If you don't, you may lose important legal rights and delay clearing your name.

Getting your credit reports, writing and disputing information with the CRAs, and then dealing with the individual creditors is critical. However, it is also straightforward. Here are the basic steps:

1. Contact all three CRAs by phone to place initial *fraud alerts* on your credit files. These last only 90 days. You will get a letter advising you of your right to a free credit report.

   Equifax: 1-888-766-0008

   Experian: 1-888-397-3742

   TransUnion: 1-800-680-7289

2. You may request an extended fraud alert on your credit profile for seven years by writing each of the credit bureaus. This alert notifies potential creditors to call you before issuing credit.

Legal Lingo

A **fraud alert** is a notation that tells anyone receiving your credit report that you're the victim of identity theft and not to issue credit without calling you first. An initial fraud alert stays on your credit file for 90 days and can be placed by phone. Extended fraud alerts, requested in writing, stay on credit files for seven years. A security freeze, requested in writing, stops potential creditors from receiving your credit file so fraudsters cannot open new accounts. You must provide a password for a credit bureau to release the report to potential creditors.

3. If you wish to lock your credit to all new potential creditors, you can call, e-mail, or write the credit bureaus to request a security freeze on your credit profile. You will receive a password from each credit reporting agency that it will require to release your credit report when you apply for new credit. Analyze the credit reports for clues as to how your identity has been stolen. (Don't worry, we'll tell you what to look for later in this chapter.)

4. Dispute the fraud in writing.

5. Contact the individual creditors, close the accounts, and get the records for those accounts.

6. Dispute the fraudulent records with the individual creditors.

This section will discuss the first two of these steps. The section titled "Warning Signs of Trouble" covers step 3. The final section, "Filing Fraud Complaints," covers steps 4, 5, and 6.

Contact the CRAs for Your Credit Reports

Your first step is to telephone each of the CRAs to place an initial fraud alert, which will entitle you to a free credit report after the alert is set, using the phone numbers listed earlier in the chapter. All three CRAs have different report formats and all three may receive different information on any one person.

Identity Crisis

Under federal law, to clear your case of identity theft, you must start by contacting the three CRAs. Whichever one you contact is supposed to contact the others to alert them of the fraud, but studies have shown that often the forwarding of the alert doesn't work, so contact all three bureaus yourself.

Follow the voice prompts to place the initial fraud alert. During the 90 days of its span, the alert requires creditors to telephone you for prior permission to create a new credit account. When you place a fraud alert, you must provide a phone number for creditors to use. I suggest that you give your cell phone number. That way if you want a credit account yourself, and you are at the creditor's place of business, you can be reached by phone. Also, if you are on vacation and a fraudster is trying to get credit, you'll know before you get home. After your call, the CRA is required to send you a letter outlining your rights, including the right to receive two credit reports for free in the next 12 months. (Some states provide more free reports.)

Write for Credit Reports and Extended Protection

Once you've received each letter from a CRA outlining your rights, you need to reply in writing (return receipt requested). You will request the following:

◆ An extension of the fraud alert from 90 days to seven years.

◆ As an alternative, you can request a credit freeze on your credit file, which involves receiving a password that will allow you to release your credit report in order for you to get credit yourself.

◆ A free copy of your credit report.

In your letter, mention your initial call date. Include a copy of your completed FTC Identity Theft Affidavit as well as a copy of your law-enforcement report, as detailed in Chapter 3. Provide the name and contact phone number of the investigator in charge of your case. Also enclose a copy of your driver's license or state identification as well as a copy of a utility bill mailed to your address as verification of your identity. You are going to ask for the following:

♦ The name and contact information for the fraud-resolution investigator in their office who will be working on your case.

♦ That an extended fraud alert be placed in your credit file for at least seven years indicating that you are a victim of fraud and that any creditor call you before issuing credit. If you prefer, you can instead ask for a security freeze to stop potential creditors from receiving your credit report, and a password to allow you to "thaw" the report to make it available to new creditors or employers

♦ That no one change the address in your credit file from your current one, which you will provide, without verification in writing from you.

♦ A complete and unedited copy of your credit report sent to your address so you may ascertain the fraud.

♦ To have your name removed from all promotional lists permanently or as provided by federal law.

♦ That the CRA inform all credit grantors and employers who have received copies of your credit report in the last year that you have been the victim of identity theft, and that the CRA provide you with the contact information of all creditors and others who have received your credit profile in the last year.

♦ A list of names, phone numbers, and addresses of all credit grantors listed on your credit file, including inquiries, so you can contact them.

♦ All documents with information on your legal rights and how to deal with the situation as well as any form or requirements for you to include a 100-word victim statement in your credit file.

Indicate that you expect to hear back from them within two weeks. Mark that date on your calendar so you can follow up if necessary.

Information = Power

Whenever a company is supposed to contact others on your behalf, request a copy of the correspondence. They often won't provide a copy, but be sure to state in writing that you have a right to such copies. In the event that you cannot clear your name, it shows their unwillingness to assist you and will provide evidence if you need to take legal action.

Understanding What's on Credit Reports

Because the majority of identity theft is undertaken for financial fraud, your credit report becomes your first line of defense. Reading your reports might seem intimidating, but don't let it frustrate you, just take your time.

Each CRA has its own formats for credit reports. However, the types of information they provide are similar. You want to particularly note a number of areas in your credit report:

- ◆ Header
- ◆ Contact box
- ◆ Credit history
- ◆ Prior payment history
- ◆ Accounts turned over to collection agencies
- ◆ Applicable courthouse records, including suits, judgments, and bankruptcies
- ◆ Your former home addresses and employers
- ◆ Inquiry sections

The header has your name, address, and other personally identifying information. The contact box gives the contact information you use in disputing the information in your credit file. Credit history is what creditors report about your accounts with them. Prior payment history shows whether you were late in paying accounts, as well as the amount and dates of your payments.

The inquiry sections are made up of two types of requests. One is from companies that want your profile as part of a regular review of an account you have with them, or from companies that buy information about you from CRAs to provide a pre-screened offer of credit. These inquiries are only seen by you, and do not affect your credit score. They are sometimes called *soft pulls*.

The other inquiry section is more important because it shows *hard pulls*, which show potential new creditors who requested your report in order to issue new accounts in your name. Other creditors see hard pulls, which affect your credit score as well. This section will show the names of the creditors and dates on which they accessed your report. This will help you understand which company issued the first fraud account, which would have enabled the fraudster to get more credit.

Legal Lingo

A **hard-pull** inquiry is a company's request for your credit report that was initiated by you or your impostor seeking to open an account, get a loan, rent an apartment, or even get a job, and it affects your credit score. A **soft pull** is either an account review of your credit profile by a company with whom you already have a relationship, or it is an indication that a company has reviewed partial information from the CRAs in order to make you a pre-screened offer. Soft pulls do not affect your credit score.

The most complex area of a credit report is the credit history, because it lists each account associated with your name, and each account shows extensive information. Here's what you'll find in the account information from all three CRAs:

Company name: Name of the company with whom you have an account.

Account number: Creditor's identifying number for the account.

Whose account: Your relationship to the account (whether individual, meaning solely in your name; joint, for accounts where you are a joint owner; or authorized user, which means that someone else owns it but you are authorized to use it).

Date opened: When the account was opened.

Months reviewed: How many months of activity the creditor has reported.

Date of last activity: Date on which the account was last used.

High credit: Largest amount of credit used on the account.

Status: Codes for the type of account.

Terms: Number of monthly installments or payments due (may be zero depending on status).

Balance: Amount owed on the account at the time reported.

Past due: Amount past due at the time reported.

Date reported: Date the creditor last reported the account to the CRA.

Once you know how to read your credit reports, it's time to look for indications that someone has stolen your identity.

Warning Signs of Trouble

There will be specific indications that you have a problem. There can be innocent explanations for any of these signs, but you need to assume that they are signs of fraud and identity theft. If you don't treat these as fraud now, you can permanently lose the right to dispute them as fraud. However, if you treat them as fraud only to learn that they actually were some type of mistake, like the CRA confusing you with someone else with a similar name (called a merged file), you preserve all your rights and there is no harm. Here's what you need to look for in each one.

Fraudulent Header Info

The header information shows your personal information, including your name, other previous names, a spouse's name, your address, previous addresses, current employer, date of birth, and Social Security number. Creditors use it to verify your information. CRAs sell some of this information to companies that can then not only send unsolicited offers of credit (unless you opt out at 888-5-OPT-OUT, which I suggest), but further sell header information to others. If any information in the header is wrong, it is a red flag for identity theft.

Look for the wrong spelling of your name, an old or unknown address, a Social Security number with one digit off, or an incorrect birthday. Do not dismiss any variance as unimportant. Fraudsters are clever and can use your name and personal data to have credit cards sent to an address in another state.

Hard Pulls on Your Data

The inquiry section that lists hard pulls shows which companies obtained your complete credit report in order to make a decision whether to issue credit.

A danger sign is hard-pull inquiries by companies that you do not recognize. It may mean that an impersonator is requesting credit in your name without your knowledge or authorization. Another red flag is an account review by a company you don't recognize. Lately fraudsters are opening business accounts in the names of their victims. A business account doesn't appear on credit reports in the account history; only consumer accounts appear in that section. Most business credit accounts are reported to Dunn & Bradstreet, but creditors who issue business accounts to you have a right to account reviews. So even if you don't see a fraudulent business account on your report, if you see an account review for a company with whom you don't have a relationship, you may have a business fraud account in your name. Chapter 13 has details on this type of fraud.

Fraudulent Accounts/Liens/Collections

Someone may have already gained and abused credit in your name. If you see an account in the credit history, a lien, or a delinquent account that has been turned over to a collection agency and know nothing of it, you probably have been defrauded. However, as I mentioned earlier, sometimes a CRA will accidentally merge your file with someone else's, so this may also be an error.

Questionable Inquiries

Remember that many third parties, including landlords as well as both current and prospective employers, can request your credit report. If you see inquiries that you can't explain, it may indicate that someone is impersonating you.

Unapproved Pre-Approvals

If your fraudster has secured credit in your name but at his or her address, then the impostor may be receiving additional pre-approved credit offers. That is why you must review the "soft pulls section" and also stop any pre-approved offers from being sent by calling 888-5-OPT-OUT, which will take you off the list of people who received pre-approved credit offers.

Once your name and creditworthiness have been sold to companies wishing to offer you credit or insurance, those companies have a year to make the offer. So your impostor may accept a preapproved offer many months after the prescreening inquiry appears on your report.

Bankruptcies

Another part of the report you want to examine is in the public-records section. Your impostor may file bankruptcy in your name to avoid eviction if he leased an apartment or foreclosure if he obtained a mortgage in your name. Look also for IRS liens if your impostor owes taxes in your name.

Filing Fraud Complaints

At this point, you will know which items on the credit report appear to be false or at least suspicious. Now you need to file a fraud *dispute* about the items with each CRA that issued a report containing fraud items.

You can dispute any item in the credit report, including accounts you didn't apply for, accounts sent to collections, liens you didn't know about, bankruptcies you didn't file, incorrect information in the credit file header, or hard pulls that you didn't authorize. You should only file a complaint for items that show solid evidence of fraud. You'll also try to get a law-enforcement agency to include all the fraud in its report.

> **Legal Lingo** _____
>
> A **dispute** means that the specific information is fraudulent and you disagree with information or an account and allege that it is incorrect. A complaint means that you have gotten a law-enforcement agency to include the information or account in an identity-theft report. Your dispute must include specific information and attachments indicating fraud.

You must write letters, return receipt requested, to the CRAs about information that is erroneous or fraudulent. You may need to write several letters to the CRAs as you learn more about the fraud or if new fraud appears. Each letter should indicate the name of the appropriate fraud dispute number and investigator whose name and contact information appears in your first correspondence received from the CRA. You need to include the following in your letter:

- ◆ Your name, Social Security number, and date of birth

- ◆ Overview of your identity theft

- ◆ Any header information that is incorrect or fraudulent

> **Information = Power** _____
>
> You may also need to dispute soft-pull inquiries if they are for account reviews for fraudulent accounts. This is especially important if a fraudster opened a business account in your name. The actual account won't appear on the report; the account review will be your only indicator—until the account goes into collection. You will need to follow up and dispute the fraudulent business account review because it enables you to use the Fair Credit Reporting Act, which usually only allows disputes of consumer personal accounts.

- ◆ All accounts for which you are filing a fraud complaint

- ◆ A copy of the law-enforcement report and the name and contact information of the law-enforcement agency

- All fraud information, including public records, that you are disputing

- All fraudulent inquiries

- A request that the agency immediately block all the fraudulent information and provide you a corrected report deleting the fraud

For all information that is fraudulent or incorrect, provide the accurate information. Specifically request the names, addresses, and telephone numbers of all the creditors you listed that issued fraudulent accounts under your name if they don't appear on the report.

In the letter, you will also provide a 100-word statement that the CRA is obliged to include in your credit file and send to any third party that requested your credit report in the last six months. In the statement, include the following:

- A sentence stating that someone has assumed your identity and received credit in your name, including the person's address, if you have found it on the credit report.

- The number of the law-enforcement report as well as the name and phone number of the investigator and agency.

- A sentence providing your current address and stating that it is not to be changed for any credit purposes or on the report without verification from you.

- A statement that credit is not to be granted in your name without verification by phone.

Under federal law, the CRA has 30 days in which to conduct an investigation of the items you list in a dispute, or 5 days for items in a fraud complaint. The CRA will contact the creditors, indicate the claim of fraud, and ask the creditors to investigate the accounts or information. If they cannot verify the accounts, the items will be permanently deleted. You will also need to notify the creditors immediately about the fraud and ask them to close the accounts and provide you evidence of the accounts, which I explain in Chapters 5 through 8.

You must also call and write third-party creditors, collection agencies, lien holders, bankruptcy courts, or others involved with the fraud and dispute with them after you first dispute the items with the CRAs. If the CRAs don't remove an item from your credit file at first because the creditor verifies the items as your true accounts, you then

Information = Power

The CRAs are not obligated to remove correct negative information from your credit report unless it is more than seven years old (10 years for bankruptcy), or it cannot verify the information with the entity who reported it. They must report back to you whether they could verify the data as true.

must prove to the creditor that the account is fraudulent. Once the creditor receives your evidence of fraud, it must notify the CRAs to remove it. However, to protect yourself, you will demand that the creditor or other entity provide you a letter that the fraud will be deleted from your credit profile so you may send a copy of the letter to the CRAs to ensure that the items are deleted permanently. Part 2 of this book has details on dealing with various kinds of third parties that report fraudulent information to the CRAs.

The Least You Need to Know

◆ Get your credit reports from all three CRAs.

◆ Place a fraud alert on your credit files immediately and follow up with a letter requesting a seven-year alert and possibly a security freeze to lock up your credit profile.

◆ Dispute all incorrect or fraudulent information on your credit reports in writing, return receipt requested.

◆ Dispute information with the CRA before or at the same time you are writing to the creditors or other entities to inform them of the fraud.

5

Credit Cards

In This Chapter

- ◆ You have rights
- ◆ Handling account-takeover fraud
- ◆ The difficulties of application fraud

If the identity thief has caused you credit-card problems, then you've either found unexplained charges on your own credit-card bills or have learned about fraudulent credit card accounts created using your personal information. You'll learn about new accounts from strange collection demands or perhaps review of your credit report.

This chapter will start with an explanation of your credit-card rights. After that, I'll separately cover the details of how to address the two types of credit-card fraud. But before you go any further, make sure you've gone through the steps in Chapter 4 to get your credit report and dispute fraudulent information as well as to place a fraud alert or credit freeze on your credit files.

Credit-Card Rights

Take a deep breath. You'll be happy to know that credit-card fraud, although rampant, is often the most straightforward fraud to cure. There are two types of credit-card fraud: *account-takeover* and *application fraud*. Each one needs different handling.

> **Legal Lingo**
>
> In **account-takeover** credit-card fraud, someone charges purchases to your own credit cards. **Application fraud** means that someone has used your identity to establish new credit-card accounts that you don't know about.
> The **Fair Credit Billing Act** is a law, passed in 1986, that changed the Truth in Lending Act to "protect the consumer against inaccurate and unfair credit billing and credit-card practices."

Just as you have rights to dispute information on your credit report, you also have rights in dealing with fraudulent credit-card charges in your name. Depending on the situation, different sets of laws can come into play.

For cases of account-takeover fraud, where someone is charging purchases to your own credit card, the applicable law is the *Fair Credit Billing Act* (FCBA). This law specifically applies to open-ended accounts like credit cards and applies to billing errors, including unauthorized charges, such as fraud.

Here are your rights and responsibilities under the law:

♦ You must dispute charges in writing.

♦ Your dispute must arrive at the creditor within 60 days of the first date that the bill(s) with the erroneous or fraudulent charges were mailed to you.

♦ The credit-card company must acknowledge your letter within 30 days of receipt. (Chapter 18 covers what to do when companies or institutions don't cooperate.)

♦ The company must resolve the dispute within two billing cycles, but not longer than 90 days, of receiving your letter.

♦ You don't have to pay the disputed or fraudulent charges during the investigation, although you must pay undisputed charges, including finance charges on accurate charges.

♦ The company cannot report you as delinquent to the CRAs, or even threaten to report derogatory information, while the matter is in dispute. However, it can report that you are challenging a bill.

♦ If the company fails to meet the statutory deadlines, then it must take the disputed charges off your account even if it thinks that the charges are legitimate.

If an account is created by the fraudster, your rights derive from the Fair Credit Billing Act and the Fair Debt Collection Practices Act, and you have major rights under the Fair Credit Reporting Act, the same law that governs how consumers deal with credit reports. Here is what you're legally entitled to from a credit-card company:

Information = Power

Under federal law, credit-card issuers must cover all but $50 of any losses that result from fraudulent credit-card charges. But the good news is all issuers will absorb the first $50 if you prove the charges are fraudulent.

♦ You have the right to dispute the account as fraudulent. You must provide a written explanation of the fraud and attach an identity-theft report. You must also complete the FTC identity-theft affidavit and provide evidence of your identity.

♦ Upon your written request, the card issuer must give you copies of the fraudulent credit-card application and copies of billing statements and correspondence regarding the bill.

♦ The issuer must provide you with this documentation within 30 days of your request and cannot charge you for it.

♦ As a victim, you may also authorize a law-enforcement investigator to receive the same records without a court order.

♦ You have a right to demand that the issuer send notice to the CRAs to remove the accounts and inquiries regarding the account from your credit reports.

Later in this chapter, I will show you how to clear the fraudulent credit-card information off your credit file.

Credit Card Account-Takeover Fraud

If you only have to deal with credit account-takeover fraud, which could happen if your credit-card information or the physical card itself was stolen—relax. It is the easiest situation to face because the FCBA gives you some powerful tools to correct the problem. (Note that this only covers credit card account-takeover, not debit card account-takeover, which I discuss in Chapter 7.)

Take the following steps:

1. Immediately review your credit-card bills as soon as they arrive by mail or online, but, at the very latest, within 30 days of receiving your credit-card bill. When you first see a fraudulent charge, contact the credit-card company by phone to alert them to any questionable charges on your bill. At that point, ask them for the address for any correspondence about fraud.

2. If there is only one charge you don't recognize, first call the vendor about the fraudulent purchase. Its phone number should be on the credit-card statement. You may not recognize the merchant account name, but the charge might still be legitimate. Ask the vendor about the charges; you'll know if its fraud or really your own purchase. If there is only one fraudulent charge, tell the credit card company, but you need not close the account.

3. If you see several charges that are clearly fraudulent, immediately call the credit-card company to ask for a new card with a new number in its place, even if you don't have all the information yet. Always replace a credit card immediately, since you may have trouble getting credit when you are a fraud victim until all is resolved. It is far easier for the issuer to send you a new card with a different number than for you to deal with the potential of continuing fraudulent charges.

4. Put a new password on the account to keep unauthorized people from gaining access.

5. The credit-card company should report to the CRAs that the account is closed due to fraud.

Identity Crisis

Remember that you're dealing with an identity thief who may have access to your personal information. Make sure you safeguard your sensitive data offline and online. Never use a password such as your mother's maiden name, child's name, and so on. Make up a nonsense word that uses at least 12 characters, including numbers, symbols, and upper- and lowercase letters.

Disputing Fraudulent Charges

Once you cancel your credit card due to fraud, the credit-card company will send you an affidavit to sign regarding the fraudulent purchases. You will need to send back the completed affidavit. Identify each fraudulent charge. The company will investigate the charges. Unless there are suspicious circumstances (such as a family member's receipt of your card at your address), you will not be held responsible for the unauthorized charges, and will not need to send any further letters. Of course, you will need to pay all the authorized charges on the billing statement.

If the company does not believe you and tries to hold you accountable for the fraudulent charges, then you will need to write a follow-up letter with the following information:

♦ A statement that you are a victim of credit-card fraud listing the identifiable fraudulent charges.

♦ A statement that you are making your request under the Fair Credit Billing Act.

♦ A demand that the charge(s) be immediately removed.

♦ A request for a copy of the company's fraud-dispute form(s), policy, and the contact information for the person who receives appeals.

♦ A request for the name and contact information of the fraud investigator who is handling your account.

♦ A request that the fraud investigator contact you.

♦ A request that copies of the purchases, including signatures and other documentation of the disputed charges, be sent to you, as well as the results of any investigation.

♦ A demand that the account be closed due to fraud and be reported as such to the CRAs.

Identity Crisis _____

Send all correspondence return-receipt requested to the address for fraud correspondence that you requested when you initially called. Don't send fraud correspondence to the billing address because your requests could be easily lost in the shuffle of the wrong department.

As I mentioned earlier in this chapter, the credit-card company has 30 days to respond to your letter and no more than 90 days to investigate and resolve the issue. That's why it's so important to keep copies of your return receipt. If you don't receive either the initial response or the results of the investigation within the specified time frames, then write the fraud investigator, return-receipt requested, and demand per the Fair Credit Billing Act that the charges be immediately removed from the account due to delay in the investigation.

Credit-Card Application Fraud

In credit-card application fraud, the credit-card issuer has opened a new account for someone pretending to be you, usually at the fraudster's address so you won't learn about the fraud until bills are delinquent and the creditor finds you. When you finally learn of a new fraudulent account, the fraud department at the issuer considers a number of possibilities:

♦ You really opened the account and are now trying to avoid responsibility for the charges on it.

♦ You may be telling the truth, but you can't prove it, which means the company will demand that you pay the bill.

♦ You're clearly a victim since the evidence is overwhelming in your favor (for example, you were in Iraq when the charges were made in Miami).

The credit-card issuer has many cases of alleged fraud and since the creditor has lost money and may have been negligent in issuing the card, you will have to face the hurdle of providing enough evidence and coming across as articulate and savvy, so the fraud department will believe your story and help you to resolve the issues.

Information = Power

Keeping a respectful and polite yet assertive demeanor, no matter how upset you may feel, will be critical in conveying the impression that your claims are legitimate. Similarly, be concise and factual.

You will need to contest the entire account because none of the transactions will be yours.

Contesting Fraudulent Accounts

To contest fraudulent credit-card accounts, you must first determine which companies have issued accounts to the fraudster. Most accounts (or collection accounts, if the original creditors sold the accounts to collection agencies) will appear on at least one of your credit reports (unless it is a business account, in which case see Chapter 13). Follow the instructions in Chapter 4 to get the name and contact information of each fraud card issuer. As you recall, after you call each of these companies, you will first write the CRAs to remove the fraud accounts from your credit report.

Your next step is to write each company or collection company that issued an account to the identity thief to provide notice that the accounts in your name are fraudulent. Include the following in the package that you send:

♦ A statement that you are the victim of identity theft, briefly stating the facts as you know them.

♦ The account number of the fraudulent account.

♦ A statement that you are disputing the account as fraudulent, as allowed by the Fair Credit Reporting Act.

♦ Attach copies of your FTC identity fraud-affidavit, law-enforcement identity-theft report, a copy of a government-issued ID, and a utility bill showing the address where you live.

♦ A demand that the account be immediately terminated, that the issuer inform all three CRAs that the account was fraudulent, and that any debt be discharged.

♦ A request for copies of the company's fraud-dispute forms and its identity-theft mitigation plan.

♦ A demand for copies of the account application, billing statements, and all documentation of the fraud account be sent within 30 days without the need for a subpoena to you and the law-enforcement agency you designate at no cost in accordance with FCRA 609e.

♦ A request for the name and contact information of the fraud investigator who will be handling your case.

♦ A statement that your current address and phone numbers, which you have included, are the only ones to use to correspond with you.

♦ A request for a written response regarding the investigation, indicating that you have disputed the account as fraudulent, that the company has discharged the debt, that the company has notified the CRAs that the account was fraudulent, and that they have removed the account and all inquiries from your credit report.

Identity Crisis

You must dispute fraudulent credit and collection accounts with the credit bureau(s) before or at the same time as you dispute the accounts with the credit-card issuers. Failure to do so will make it difficult to legally challenge the credit bureaus if they refuse to delete the fraud from your credit profile.

As always, be sure to send all correspondence by certified mail, return receipt requested. The card issuer can ask you to use its own affidavit form, but should not require you to have it notarized unless it is willing to pay for the notary. You can substitute signatures of witnesses for notarization if you choose. Or you can get your bank's verification of your signature, which Chapter 3 discusses.

Delay and Deny

The issuer has 30 days in which to investigate your claims and respond to them. If you don't hear back, call the fraud department, and then send a follow-up letter, requesting a resolution, with a copy of your receipt showing that your letter was received by the company.

If the issuer sends you a letter stating that the account is legitimate and that it denies the fraud claim and verifies the account with the credit bureaus, you will need to call whoever sent you the denial letter, and ask for a higher authority to appeal that decision. Here are some types of evidence that should prove that the account was fraudulent for your appeal:

◆ Signature on the account application and erroneous information on the application, such as an incorrect birth date or mother's maiden name

◆ Fraudulent addresses used

◆ Types of merchandise ordered and the address where the packages were sent

◆ In-person transactions occurring at a combination of time and place where you can prove you were elsewhere

The Least You Need to Know

◆ There are two different types of credit-card fraud and several federal laws that will help you clear your name.

◆ You have rights that you must exert in writing.

◆ Account-takeover credit-card fraud is easy to fix usually with a phone call and one affidavit.

◆ New account application credit-card fraud challenges you to prove the fraud with extensive evidence.

Chapter 6

Other Fraud on Credit Reports

In This Chapter

- ◆ Handling fraudulent accounts listed on your credit report
- ◆ Dealing with falsified loans
- ◆ Dealing with sham department store accounts
- ◆ How to stop a collection agency

When it comes to credit identity theft, there are two fundamental types of financial frauds: those that immediately show up on your credit report, and those that only appear when a company has reported an account to a collection agency.

This chapter focuses on accounts or obligations, other than credit cards (Chapter 5 covers those), that someone creates under your name, that require a credit check, and that report to CRAs. Chapters 7 and 8 detail how to handle the fraud that will not appear on your credit reports.

Non-Credit Card Fraud on Your Credit Report

This chapter covers three major types of identity-theft financial fraud:

- Falsified loans

- Sham department store accounts

- Fraudulent accounts that have been sold to a collection agency

Your clue that someone has been using your name to get loans and credit will be suspicious items on one or more of your credit reports. Using the credit report is critical because usually the fraudster will create accounts with his or her own address or a mailing service, so you won't get copies of bills. See Chapter 4 for details of how to get your credit report, how to read it, and how to dispute fraudulent information in it.

Information = Power

Under no circumstances should you *ever* pay bills that the identity thief incurred in your name. Doing so will make it difficult to prove that the debt isn't yours, and will leave you with a bad credit report for years.

If you act immediately upon learning of the fraud, you can probably avoid all financial liability—once you prove that you're innocent and take appropriate action. Following is the basic pattern you're going to follow to clear up the fraud and your name.

First, dispute the loans or accounts with the CRAS that listed the fraud. Demand that the CRA remove the fraudulent account from your credit record. The CRA will undertake an investigation. If you don't first dispute the account with the CRA, the CRA will not have a duty to force the creditor to investigate. It may be difficult for you to delete the fraudulent account from your credit profile if the creditor doesn't believe that you are a victim of identity theft. Chapter 4 has detailed instructions for how to do this.

The CRAs will communicate your fraud claims to the lender or account issuer for verification. The creditor has a duty then to investigate. If the creditor verifies to the CRA that the debt is legitimate, you have a right to demand in writing (return-receipt requested) that the creditor (whose contact information is on the credit report) provide you evidence of the investigation. You will dispute the account as fraudulent, provide your FTC affidavit, law-enforcement report, and evidence of your identity, and ask for copies of the fraudulent application, billing statements, and all other correspondence.

If the creditor sends you a letter stating that the account is not accepted as fraud, you will need to contact the person who sent the letter and ask for the next higher-up person and prepare to prove your innocence. If you continue to have a problem, see Chapter 18.

> **Information = Power**
>
> The process of challenging a collection agency is a little different than dealing directly with other creditors. Once you inform them of the deception and provide them written evidence, they must notify the original creditor that the account is disputed as fraud. The last section of this chapter explains what to do.

In the case of illegitimate loans or department store accounts, here is what you need to do:

1. Call the telephone number of the entity listed in your credit report. If the phone number is not listed, search for it online. Should that fail, call the CRA for the contact information.

2. Ask to speak to the fraud department. If there is no fraud department, speak to the billing department. Concisely relate the situation to the representative and ask for the name and address of the person to whom you should write about the fraud.

3. Write a letter to document your conversation.

In the letter you send to the fraud or billing department contact, include the following:

♦ A statement that you are the victim of identity theft with a brief list of the facts as you know them.

♦ The account number of the fraudulent account.

♦ A statement that you are disputing the account as fraudulent as allowed by the Fair Credit Reporting Act, and that you have disputed the account with the CRAs.

♦ Copies of your FTC identity fraud affidavit and your law-enforcement identity-theft report.

◆ Copies of a government-issued ID and of a utility bill showing your home address.

◆ A demand that the account be immediately terminated, that the issuer inform all three CRAs that the account was fraudulent, and that any debt be discharged.

◆ A request for a copy of the company's fraud-dispute forms and information regarding its identity-theft mitigation plan.

◆ A demand that copies of the account application, billing statements, tax returns purporting to be yours (often provided to lenders), and all correspondence between the impostor and the entity to be sent to you and the law enforcement agency you designate at no cost to you within 30 days without the need for a subpoena in accordance with FCRA 609e.

◆ A request for the name and contact information of the fraud investigator who will be handling your case.

◆ A statement that your current address and phone numbers, including cell phone, are the only ones to use to correspond with you.

◆ A request for a written response regarding the investigation within 30 days, indicating that you have disputed the account as fraudulent and that the company has discharged the debt and notified the CRAs to remove the account and all inquiries from your credit report.

If you don't hear back, call the fraud department again, and ask to speak to a supervisor. Then send a follow-up letter documenting the conversation, and request a resolution. Include a copy of your return receipt showing that your original letter was received by the company.

Information = Power _____

If the issuer sends you a letter stating that it denies the fraud claim, you will need to call whoever sent you the denial letter and ask for a higher authority to appeal that decision. You may also call to complain to the FTC at 1-877-IDTHEFT or complete a form online at www.ftc.gov/bcp/edu/microsites/idtheft/consumers/form-filling-instructions.html. Chapter 18 has more information about what to do with particularly "prickly" creditors.

Falsified Loans

Three types of loans are by far the most common in identity-theft cases:

- ◆ Student loans/student aid
- ◆ Car or boat loans
- ◆ Mortgages or other home loans

Here are some special considerations for each one.

Student Loans and Student Aid

An impostor may have applied for a student loan or student aid under your name and Social Security number. A bank, a private institution, or the government will have issued it, in which case you proceed as described previously.

In addition to the institution that provided the loan, you may find out that there was aid or a scholarship as well, which could impede your ability to get a scholarship yourself and may affect you in insidious ways later. You will need to contact the U.S. Department of Education Inspector General's Hotline at 1-800-MIS-USED (800-647-8733).

Identity Crisis

Although some student-loan fraud is committed to get the available cash for purposes other than education, there have been cases in which impostors have received degrees using the victims' names. Victims are then saddled with loans to repay for the education of their impersonators.

To prove your innocence, you should consider the following types of evidence:

- ◆ Comparisons of the signature on the loan application as well as information on the application, such as a birth date or mother's maiden name, that might be incorrect.

- ◆ Fraudulent addresses and fake school records.

◆ An educational institution located unrealistically far from your true home, making commuting impossible.

◆ Comparisons of tax returns sent to the lender and your true tax return.

Sometimes student-loan fraud is perpetrated by someone who knew you in the past, for example someone who attended high school with you or a previous neighbor. If this is the case, see Chapter 11, which has details on how to handle identity theft by friends.

Car or Boat Loans

Although you handle a fraudulent car or boat loan as shown earlier in this chapter, either can indicate that the fraudster has obtained government identification, like a driver's license, in your name. If so, Chapter 12 covers that topic in detail.

To prove your innocence once you have received documents from the lender, you should consider the following types of evidence:

◆ The copy of the driver's license retained by the car or boat dealership.

◆ Signature on the account application and erroneous information on the application, such as bank account numbers, birth date, other lenders you don't recognize.

◆ Fraudulent addresses, impostor co-borrowers, the registration for a vehicle or boat, or on any government identification that the criminal may have obtained.

Mortgages or Home Loans

This type of identity theft requires that you contact many more entities to help you prove to the lender that the mortgage was illegitimate.

Start by contacting the lender listed in the credit report and get a copy of the entire loan file, including all the information and paperwork associated with the original application. You will also need to get documents from mortgage broker if there was one, the escrow company that handled the purchase, the notary who verified signatures, the title company that insured the property, and the real-estate agents that were involved.

If you have telephoned the lender, follow up in writing as described in this chapter. The loan file will identify the various involved parties. If a deed for the property was recorded in your name, you'll need to get a copy of it from the city or county in which it was recorded, which is also where the property is located.

Information = Power

If your mortgage identity theft was a conspiracy by some of the professionals involved in the transaction to defraud the lender, there may be several criminals involved. Hopefully, the lender will encourage the FBI to investigate and assist in the process.

You will need to work with the lender about tendering the deed quickly, especially if foreclosure has begun. You don't want a foreclosure on your record. Depending on the circumstances, you may need to hire a real-estate lawyer to assist you. However, if the lender was negligent in issuing the loan, you may be able to recoup your legal fees and more.

The identity thief who obtained the fraudulent home loan may be living in the home, but don't pay the person a visit, as it could be dangerous. It is also possible that the thief does not live there, but instead has leased the property to an innocent person, or even sold it. You won't know until you investigate the situation and involve law enforcement.

To prove the loan doesn't belong to you, here are questions to ask when reviewing the loan-application package:

- Does information on the loan application, including payroll and tax documents, match your circumstances?

- Does address information on W-2 forms, paystubs, or tax returns match the victim's address?

- Are paystubs computer-generated, and can the employer verify or provide more information about the impostor?

- Is the fraudster's employer's address noted on the verification of employment?

- Is the employer within a logical distance of the subject property?

- Do account statements indicate deposits of employment income as evidenced by file?

- For verbal verification of employment, was the employer's phone number independently verified using 411, a drive-by visit, or a similar way?

- Does the fraudster occupy the property, or did the person intend to either rent it out or sell it?

- If absent, did the impostor intend to rent the residence with a documented lease or sell the property?

- Does the owner of the property match the owner on the title and sales contract? On the property title?

- Did the fraudster execute the contract with another person?

- Are Realtors, escrow agents, or notaries involved in the scam, or can they provide help?

- Does the fraudster signature match other file documents?

- Does the title policy list lien holders that are to be paid?

- Has a warranty deed been filed on the property versus a quitclaim deed?

Once you can answer these questions from your analysis of the loan documents, then you have substantial evidence to substantiate in a phone call and follow-up letter to prove the fraud to the lender. It's quite a bit to unravel, however; the lender must help you and the title company will be on the hook and should investigate as well. There are many legal issues that you should discuss with an attorney, as Chapter 18 discusses.

Department Stores

A department store revolving credit account is generally handled directly by the company's business office. Call the billing number to dispute the account as explained earlier in this chapter. In addition to asking in writing for a copy of the account application and billing statements from the store, you should also ask for copies of signed charge slips and any correspondence.

What makes revolving credit accounts different from loans is that they are generally tied to multiple purchases. In addition to the usual proof of innocence, there are the following:

- ◆ Signature on account application

- ◆ Erroneous personal information on the account

- ◆ Fraudulent address

These accounts will also have records of purchases. The charges on the billing statement should show the department where the item was purchased. Try contacting that department to find out who the salesperson was for the purchase. If, for example, your fraudster went to Victoria's Secret often, perhaps the salesperson will be able to distinguish your impostor from your photo.

Information = Power

The address of the impersonator will clearly show your address is different. Purchase records will help prove that you were somewhere else at that time that the impostor was in the store. The purchases themselves are evidence. In addition, the signature on the charge slip will clearly not be yours.

Collection Agencies

You may have found that one or more creditors has sold fraudulent accounts to collection agencies, who then contacted you, or you saw collection accounts on your credit report.

You have additional rights under the *Fair Debt Collection Practices Act*, and the Fair Credit Reporting Act, including the ability to demand the following:

As a victim under the FCRA, once you notify orally and in writing the collection agency, it must do the following:

- ◆ Notify the original creditor that you have indicated it is a fraudulent account.

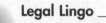

Legal Lingo _____

The **Fair Debt Collection Practices Act** is a federal law that governs how debt collectors can collect debts. It does not affect the internal collection departments of creditors, only independent organizations that purchase uncollectable debt from companies at a discount and try to collect the debt to earn a profit.

◆ If you request so in writing, provide you all documentation they have of the account.

◆ Stop collections activity.

◆ Require that the original creditor repurchase the debt as fraudulent.

In addition, the collection agency must provide you with the following on your written request:

◆ Written notice of the amount of a debt.

◆ The name and address of the original creditor.

◆ A statement that you have 30 days to dispute the validity of the debt.

◆ Documentation and verification of the debt.

You also have the right to demand that the original creditor not resell the fraudulent account to a debt-collection agency. If you receive a phone call from a collection agency, tell them of the fraud, and demand written notice, which the agency is obliged to give you within five days. Once you receive the written notice, you have 30 days to write your letter, provide the FTC affidavit and police report, ask for the documentation, and demand that they no longer attempt collection. You will also need to immediately dispute the collection account with the CRAs.

When sending a letter (return receipt requested) to the collection agency, include everything you would for any credit report–listed debt as described earlier in this chapter. In addition, you want to add the following:

- A demand for the name, address, and phone number of the original creditor

- A demand that, because the debt is fraudulent, all collection activity immediately stop and that the collection agency sell back the account to the creditor

- A demand for all documents of the account in the possession of the collection agency pursuant to FCRA 609e

Then write the original creditor, using a letter with attachments as described earlier in this chapter, to challenge the account as fraudulent and the result of identity theft. Also remind the creditor not to re-sell the account to collectors.

The Least You Need to Know

- Dispute department store accounts and loan accounts with CRAs similarly to disputing fraudulent bank-issued credit cards.

- When it comes to identity theft, collection agencies are governed by the Fair Debt Collection Practices Act and also the Fair Credit Reporting Act.

- Most loan applications require more extensive information that can help you prove your innocence, so demand that it be provided to you under FCRA 609e.

Chapter 7

Take It to the Financial Institution

In This Chapter

◆ Getting burned at the bank

◆ Dealing with check fraud

◆ Recovering from debit-card fraud

◆ Fixing investment identity theft

Some financial fraud accounts won't appear on your credit report until they are reported to debt collectors. You may have noticed bank funds depleted by an unexplained check or debit-card withdrawal. Your bank statement might show fees for bounced checks caused by mysterious transfers or sales from investment accounts. Various laws cover the different types of fraud in this chapter, and your fraud recovery actions may be multifaceted.

When it comes to banks and credit unions, there are several types of identity fraud. For example, criminals get your bank-account number or your debit-card number and make purchases or electronic transfers so that money you expected to use for your obligations may be gone. Impostors may create new checks, forged cashier's checks, or money orders in your name using your account numbers.

Information = Power

It's surprisingly easy for criminals to access your funds in your bank or credit cards. They can steal your blank checks or create new checks using the account and routing numbers they copy from the bottom of a check you use to pay a bill. It isn't even necessary to use your name or bank name on the check to draw from your account. Banks virtually never verify anything but signatures or information other than the bank numbers on the bottom of the check. And a fraudster can use the number on your debit card without needing a pin number.

In another type of bank fraud, the criminal opens a new account using your name and Social Security number. This chapter discusses each bank fraud separately. There is also a section devoted to investment-account fraud, whether a 401(k), a pension, or some other specialized type of investment vehicle.

Check and Electronic Fraud

When an identity thief has invaded your bank account through check or fraudulent electronic transfer, you'll see unexplained charges on your bank statements. Your bank statements may have stopped arriving if the fraudster has changed the address on the account. Most likely the fraudster will work to quickly drain your account. So check your online statement at least twice a week to catch the thief. Even better, set up bank e-mail alerts to see any fraud transfers immediately.

Check Your Checks

Check fraud is rampant. Fraudsters can steal your checks and use them; take checks you've written and wash off the name, replacing it with ones they are using; simply get your bank to change your address to theirs; work with an unscrupulous insider at the bank to add their name to your account; open a new account under your name or just Social Security number; or simply create counterfeit checks with your account number but someone else's name by using software purchased at a retail store. Suddenly your account is out of money or merchants are refusing to take your checks.

Check fraud can be a difficult problem to fix for a number of reasons, including the following:

- There is no universal way for merchants to verify if the check is legitimate, even if they can see if they have had a problem with your account before.

- No federal law limits how much you can lose if your checking account is depleted by fraudulent checks and you don't act immediately.

- Most states have laws granting you rights, including holding banks responsible for fraudulent transactions, but you must research them, as Chapter 1 describes.

- To deal with bad checks, you may have to deal with your bank, the bank the fraudster used, and any merchant that accepted a fraudulent check.

- The crook might be sending out bogus checks for an account you already closed, which won't matter to the merchants who contact you for payment.

- The impostor may create checks that use your account number but not your name.

- The thief may have used your name to open accounts in banks unknown to you, perhaps in another state.

If you think someone has been accessing your checking or bank accounts through stolen, newly created, or forged checks, the first step is to read Chapter 3 and file a law-enforcement identity-theft report as well as prepare an identity-theft affidavit.

Identity Crisis —————————————————

Check fraud can escalate to lawsuits and even criminal prosecution if the amounts are large enough, and if you don't immediately take steps to protect yourself. Run a background check as described in Chapter 3 (or go to www.privacyrights.org/background-checks-and-workplace). If it indicates criminal activity, check Chapter 15. If there is a civil suit, see Chapter 16.

Notify the Bank

It is critical that you examine your bank statements. Most banks will accept claims of account fraud for only 30 or 60 days after the date of the statement. If you don't inform the bank immediately, you may never get your money returned. Once you know you're the victim of identity theft, check your bank statements at least once a week if you have on-line banking. Contact the bank by phone immediately and then follow up in writing, return receipt requested. Include the following:

◆ A statement that you are the victim of identity theft with a brief list of the facts as you know them.

◆ Your bank-account number.

◆ The check numbers and respective amounts that are fraudulent and a statement that they are fraudulent. (You may print a copy of your online statement and circle the fraudulent charges.)

◆ Copies of your FTC identity-fraud affidavit and your law-enforcement identity-theft report.

◆ Copies of a government-issued ID and a utility bill showing your home address.

◆ A demand that the bank immediately close the account (if the bank did not do that when you were talking to a representative), as well as any connected or linked accounts and any associated credit cards or debit cards.

◆ A demand that a new account be opened with a security code and an ATM card with a new pin, and that funds withdrawn by the fraud be returned and deposited in the newly created account, and that all other accounts of yours receive a security code.

◆ A demand that the bank put a stop payment on any checks that may have been stolen.

◆ A request for the original check if available, or for a substitute copy if the original has been destroyed as allowed under *Check 21*.

Information = Power

A federal program called **Check 21** allows banks to transmit electronic images of a deposited check to get paid, rather than shipping the actual paper version. You get certain legal rights, like being able to have up to $2,500 in funds returned to your account within 10 days if a check is cashed in error. To exercise those rights, you'll need the original check or a substitute copy from the bank. The single-sheet copies of multiple checks that some banks send in your monthly bank statement do not give you the same rights. You must have a copy of both the front and the back of the check. If you have online banking and can print a copy of the front and back of the check image, that should serve as a substitute check.

◆ A request that the bank ask any bank that received a fraudulent check as a deposit to keep the original rather than destroying it.

◆ A request for the name and contact information of the fraud investigator who will be handling your case along with a case number, if any.

◆ A statement that your current address and phone numbers, which you have included, are the only ones to use to correspond with you.

◆ A request for written confirmation from the bank that all this has been done and that the account has been marked "closed due to theft and not to be reopened."

◆ A request that your bank notify all *check-verification companies* of the fraud.

Once you've done this, be sure to shred any blank checks that you still have from the account as well as any ATM or debit card. You will need to open a new bank account and get a new ATM, not a debit card (for reasons I explain later in the chapter). Add a password other than your mother's maiden name so no one can change any of the information, including name and address.

Notify the Check-Verification Companies

You need to report the fraudulent use of your checks to the various check-verification companies and ask them to place a fraud alert on your name and account number. Create a password to be used for any future communications. Place a "security freeze" on your consumer report, which will prohibit a check-verification company from releasing any information in your consumer file without your express authorization. If you go to open an account, the bank will receive a message indicating that you have blocked your information and you will need to authorize the inquiry. Here are the major check-verification companies and their telephone numbers:

- ◆ ChexSystems: 1-800-428-9623 www.consumerdebt.com (for identity-theft dispute form)

- ◆ Certegy/CPRS: 1-800-437-5120

- ◆ SCAN: 1-800-262-7771

- ◆ TeleCheck: 1-800-710-9898

You will want to request the free copy of your consumer file available under the FCRA. The reports will tell you if someone has been writing bad checks in your name. You will also see the names of merchants who subscribe to the service that received bad checks. Using the same type of letter as you would send in Chapter 5, dispute the fraudulent transactions and ask that they be removed.

Notify the Merchants

If someone has stolen your identity and committed check fraud, it was to get merchandise or services from merchants without any intent to pay. So the chances are good that there are companies thinking that you owe them money.

After you've received the reports from the check-verification companies, you'll have the names of at least some of the merchants that have received bad checks. Not all businesses subscribe to check-verification services, but the substitute copies of the bad checks from your bank will show who received them.

Call the billing or fraud department of the merchant that received the fraudulent checks. Ask which check-verification company the merchant uses so you may notify it, place a fraud alert, and get a free report. Write the usual follow-up letter informing it about the details of the check fraud, including whether the checks were forged or the criminal got a fraudulent account using your Social Security number. Make a copy of the entire package you sent to the bank and send it, return receipt requested, to the merchant as well so it can correct its records.

It's important to let the merchant know of the situation to keep it from continuing to report the bad checks to other check-verification companies, forcing you to spend more time and energy repeating the steps above.

Debit-Card Danger

Debit cards may look like credit cards, but different laws govern them and they don't offer the same protections to consumers. It is far more difficult to deal with debit-card fraud than credit-card fraud. When you use a credit card, you create a debt obligation for future payment. You receive a billing statement either in the mail or online and you have the opportunity to dispute charges.

However, when you use a debit card, the bank puts a hold on the amount of money immediately, usually taking it out of your checking account within a day. The fraudster will get the funds before you have time to dispute it. Someone can use your debit-card number online, by phone, or by fax without a PIN and without the card present. Instead of being governed by the Fair Credit Billing Act and Fair Credit Reporting Act, debit-card purchases are really electronic checks that only come under the *Electronic Funds Transfer Act* (EFT) when used with a PIN.

Your rights and obligations under the act include the following:

- ◆ If you report a loss within two days of learning about it, you are limited to personal loss of $50.

- ◆ If you report the loss in greater than two days but under 60, you're responsible for up to $500.

- ◆ If you wait longer than 60 days, you could lose everything that was taken out of your account.

If you report the loss in a timely manner, your bank will investigate. Although it may refund you the money temporarily, I have heard from dozens of victims that the bank often pulls the money out of the newly created account because the bank does not believe the victim.

Notify your bank immediately of any fraud, by phone, online, or in person at a branch. Make sure you get the name of the person you spoke with and his employee number, and then follow up by fax and mail, return receipt requested. Include the following:

- ◆ A statement that you are the victim of identity theft with a list of the facts as you know them.

- ◆ Your bank-account number.

- The EFT transactions on a statement that you are disputing (most easily found through online banking).

- Copies of your FTC identity-fraud affidavit and your law-enforcement identity-theft report.

- Copies of a government-issued ID and a utility bill showing your home address.

- A demand that the bank immediately close the account, if it didn't do so when you spoke to a representative, as well as any connected or linked accounts and associated credit cards or debit cards.

- A demand that the bank open a new account, refund the defrauded funds into it, add new passwords and a security code, and issue you a new ATM card.

- A request for the name and contact information of the fraud investigator who will be handling your case.

- A statement that your current address and phone numbers, which you have included, are the only ones to use to correspond with you.

Because of the stringent liability time requirements, if this is the first indication of identity theft, you may not yet have the law-enforcement identity-theft report. In that case, send the letter without the identity-theft report. However, indicate that you will file a report with a law-enforcement agency and will forward a copy when available.

Money Order and Bank Check Fraud

With the power of personal computers and ink jet printers, it's easy for criminals to forge money orders and bank or cashier checks. Even though these fake financial instruments don't involve your bank-account number, the crooks might decide to list you as the payor. When recipients find that payment has bounced, they look for you, not the fraudsters.

Treat this type of case as though it were regular check fraud. Using the steps in the previous section of this chapter, dispute the case with the check-verification services, the bank from which the check or money

order was supposedly drawn, and the merchant that received the fraudulent payment.

Fraudulent New Bank Accounts

Fraudulent checks and electronic transfers from your own bank account
are a nightmare, but at least you have a relationship with the bank and
so can get statements and evidence of what has happened.

What is more menacing is when your impostor creates bank or credit-
union accounts under your name and Social Security number, possibly with money stolen from another victim. The fraudster is using an
address where he or she has access to the statements and you don't. You
don't know about the fraud until the scammer has moved on to another
victim and siphoned or laundered the money. Eventually the bank,
looking for the person responsible, pulls the credit report for your
Social Security number and gets your contact information.

This type of fraud is particularly difficult to catch because bank accounts don't appear in a credit report, even as an inquiry, until someone
initiates collection or legal action. You may learn of it when merchants
contact you about bounced checks
when stores won't take your own
checks, or when you are unable
to open a new bank account.
The first step to correcting
the problem is to contact the
check-verification companies, as
explained earlier in this chapter,
and place a fraud alert to avoid letting the fraudster create yet other
accounts in your name.

Information = Power

Although check-verification
companies keep records of
bad checks, they do not all
track inquiries from banks that
might give advanced warning
on a criminal trying to establish
a new account in your name.

The reports, particularly one from ChexSystems, may give you a variety of types of information that will be useful, including the following:

◆ Reports from banks about outstanding debts and accounts that
have been mishandled.

◆ Inquiries from banks initiated by consumer action—that is, by
someone applying for a credit card or bank account.

- Inquiries by current creditors, creditors looking for pre-approval for an offer, potential employers, and potential investors.

- Reports by merchants of returned checks.

- History of check orders placed during the last three years.

Contact each of the institutions and businesses that have reported a returned check as well as any bank that made an inquiry initiated by consumer action when you didn't try to establish a new account. Dispute each account using the procedure earlier in this chapter.

Investment Fraud

In an investment account—whether a pension plan, a 401(k) or other individual retirement account, or a Health Savings Account—the signs of trouble are similar to those of check fraud. Either there is unexplained activity on your account, whether buying, selling, or transferring funds to another institution (some crooks use account-takeover tactics to launder dirty money and leave you with the blame); your broker contacts you about a problem; or you've stopped receiving your statements, which indicates that someone may have changed the address and diverted your account.

Information = Power

Problems with a Health Savings Account may indicate a broader issue of medical identity theft (see Chapter 14). Investment fraud is often committed by an unscrupulous insider in the company, a trusted financial planner, or a family member or associate with access to personal information necessary to make it possible (see Chapter 11). Pension plan or 401(k) fraud may be a sign of workplace identity theft (Chapter 13) or cyber identity theft, if the breach may be due to online trading accounts and cyber identity theft (see Chapter 17).

Investment fraud requires a somewhat different procedure to fix than bank-account fraud. You must work with two major types of institutions: plan administrators and securities brokerage firms.

Call your normal contact for the account, whether a benefits plan administrator at work or the contact person listed on your statement or on the broker's website, to warn of the identity theft. Close the account and open a new one on the phone. If that isn't possible for some reason, freeze the account. Ask for a copy of the procedures to resolve identity theft and get money refunded to you. You might also find information about procedures on the brokerage firm's site.

Follow the procedures, always sending materials by mail, return receipt requested. Investments are not FDIC insured but many companies have private insurance for fraud. You don't have the protection of the FCRA for security fraud, but act as though you do, demanding an investigation and refund. Include the same evidence of fraud, including law-enforcement report and identity-theft victim affidavit, as you would for an FCRA-covered creditor, as described in Chapter 6. You then contact each of the individual securities brokers or dealers. You may not be the only one experiencing this fraud, so I suggest you also contact your local FBI and Secret Service offices.

Hidden Agenda

Virtually all dealers require customers to sign an agreement that, in the case of a dispute, both the customer and the broker agree to submit themselves to arbitration under FINRA, the Financial Industry Regulatory Authority. If you cannot get a satisfactory resolution, go online to www.finra.org and click the Arbitration & Mediation link for more information on how dispute resolution works. You may also file a complaint with the Securities and Exchange Commission (www.sec.gov/complaint.shtml) if you have trouble getting your funds returned to you as a result of identity theft.

To prevent continuing fraud, set up online access to your investment accounts so you can check their status several times a month and reduce the time between the occurrence of fraud and your reporting of it. This becomes particularly important if your account only sends quarterly reports.

The Least You Need to Know

◆ Check fraud and debit-card fraud result in money drained from your account before you can prevent it.

◆ Although the FCRA doesn't cover check or debit-card fraud, use similar processes to get access to information, dispute it, and demand the timely return of your funds.

◆ Report any check fraud to the check-verification companies, the banks, and the merchants.

◆ For investment fraud, review your accounts online and close or freeze affected accounts.

Chapter 8

Discovering Hidden Fraudulent Accounts

In This Chapter

- ◆ Look for hidden signs of fraud
- ◆ Find non-credit fraud information from free consumer reports
- ◆ Discover and resolve employment and insurance fraud

Chapter 7 covered several types of financial institution fraud that doesn't appear in your credit report. I call this hidden fraud because it is financial identity theft and yet it doesn't jump out at you from your credit reports unless you know the early warning signs.

Look for the Sneaky Signs

Now we will deal with other financial fraud that may not appear on consumer reports:

◆ Cell-phone accounts

◆ Apartment leases

◆ Utility bills

◆ Gasoline credit cards

◆ Scam employment

◆ Insurance fraud

What makes these types of financial fraud harder to sort out is that when these types of companies grant new credit, they don't report active accounts to the CRAs. Such entities as cell phone carriers, land-lords, utility companies, and specialty retailers like the gasoline companies will initially check credit records with a CRA when setting up an account. However, they won't report back to the CRAs once an account is opened. With your permission or your impostor's consent (which companies take as yours anyway), many employers will inquire into your credit history as part of the hiring process.

Information = Power

I include scam employment here because there are identity thieves who will pass themselves off as you to get a job or to set up a business. Chapter 13 covers a variety of workplace fraud.

Because some creditors don't report monthly account activity to the CRAs, those fraud accounts won't show up in the credit-history section of the report, so at first glance you might think that you're safe.

However, your credit report will give you a big tip-off to these types of fraud if you look closely. Remember from Chapter 4 that there is an "inquiries" section of your credit report. There are two types of inquiries. Soft inquiries, or soft pulls, are account reviews that companies are allowed to do when they have a relationship with you (or your impostor). Hard inquiries, or hard pulls, are always initiated by a creditor or a prospective employer who believe they have permission to check your entire credit profile because of a credit application you (or your impostor) have submitted.

Investigate the hard pulls carefully. If any company unfamiliar to you has received your credit reports, there's a good chance that a fraudster passed himself or herself off as you. Detection of an unauthorized inquiry on your credit record helps you to fix the problem early. Here are the steps to take:

1. Order your free credit report (after placing a fraud alert) from all three CRAs using the steps in Chapter 4.

2. If you find unauthorized inquiries either as an account review from a company that you don't know, or from the section that shows a company accessed your report in order to issue new credit, immediately call the company to find out why the company reviewed your report. If the phone number of the company doesn't appear on the report, look it up online or contact the credit bureau for the contact information.

3. While on the phone, after learning why the hard-pull inquiry appeared on your credit profile, get the mailing address of the entity's fraud department and write a follow-up letter saying that you did not authorize the inquiry. In the letter, tell them not to issue an account to the fraudster. Ask for a copy of the application and any billing statements, and closure of the account if one was already initiated so you can stop the fraud before it proceeds to collections.

4. Also follow up in writing with the CRAs. Dispute each fraudulent hard inquiry with the CRAs. If account reviews are for fraudulent accounts, ask that they be removed. Your credit score is affected by "hard pulls," so you must remove the scam inquiries.

5. Dispute each unauthorized inquiry with the creditor, demanding all available information, as you would for fraudulent accounts that show up on the account history section of your credit report, as Chapter 6 explains. Demand that the company or individual report back to the CRA, indicating that the inquiry it made was based on a fraudulent request from an identity thief and that it should be deleted from your record.

Once you review the application and correspondence the fraudster supplied to the company, you can file an amended law-enforcement identity-theft victim report, as explained in Chapter 3. Close the fraud account if opened, prevent collections, and stop the impostor's further use.

Identity Crisis

You must dispute the inquiry with the CRAs for two additional reasons. One is that by doing so at the start, you preserve all your rights under the Fair Credit Reporting Act. The other is because these inquiries show up on the report issued to any third party, lending credence to those accounts.

Detecting Utility and Telephone Fraud

At the time of writing, most telecommunications and utility companies do not report account information to the credit bureaus. However, many report negative information to the National Consumer Telecom and Utilities Exchange, Inc.

NCTUE is a database owned by member telecommunications and utility companies that provides information on new, defaulted, or fraudulent accounts. Because, as its website (www.nctue.com) says, "it provides access to current contact information on defaulted consumers and customized treatment and collection strategies for customers who have unpaid final bills," and because Equifax, one of the three major CRAs, manages the database for NCTUE, I think this database is a "specialty consumer reporting agency" as defined under the Fair Credit Reporting Act FCRA Section 603(d).

Because any fraudulent information in this database is shared with others and would negatively impact your ability to get utilities or telephone accounts, request a free copy of your file as a victim under the FCRA as Chapter 4 explains. You should also be able to delete fraudulent information about you in those files and have NCTUE and Equifax notify the reporting companies of the fraud. You should also be able to get a list of names, phone numbers, and addresses of any entities that accessed fraudulent data associated with your name so that you may contact them to clear your name and exert all your other rights under FCRA. If you are concerned about fraudulent or erroneous activity being reported through NCTUE, contact NCTUE:

NACM Southwest
P.O. Box 167688
Irving, TX, 75016-7688

You can also telephone 972-518-0019 or e-mail nctue@equifax.com, again using the steps for CRAs from Chapter 4.

If your impostor has opened accounts with utilities, be aware that he or she may have an apartment or house lease, or has applied for and received a mortgage, in your name. Notify the landlord and all entities involved by phone and in writing to clear your name. If the impersonator has an apartment or is living in a residence in your name, you will need to contact the law-enforcement agency where the fraudster is living and ask for an investigation. If you live in a different state, you may be able to get the FBI or Secret Service involved if the crook has crossed state lines. Never call or visit the impostor yourself, since he or she may be dangerous.

ChoicePoint: Another Source of Information

A credit report can give hints, but not all financial fraud will even show up on inquiries. What if an employer doesn't run a credit check? And many insurance companies don't check a credit report before writing policies, so the inquiry section may not be helpful to your insurance fraud investigation.

But another resource may be helpful: a website called ChoicePoint. com, owned by major information brokerage LexisNexis. ChoicePoint sells background check information and consumer reports to employers, law enforcement, governmental agencies, and others. ChoicePoint, like many other data brokers, is subject to the provisions of FCRA. ChoicePoint will provide you with three types of free data reports with information about you that is subject to the information disclosure mandated by the Fair Credit Reporting Act. The three reports are as follows:

- ◆ Insurance claims history, or C.L.U.E. report
- ◆ Employment history or ChoicePoint Workplace Solutions report
- ◆ Tenant history, or Resident Data report

You can obtain free copies of each report once a year by going to the online site. Look for the "Reports About You" section and then click on the "FACT Act" link. There are instructions for getting each of the reports. You can also order your free public records search and a complete background check for a fee at www.choicepoint.com to see if there are any other illegal uses of your identity. The company's consumer assistance center toll-free number is 1-888-497-0011.

Information = Power

There may not be a ChoicePoint Workplace Solutions report for you if you haven't worked for others, a C.L.U.E. report if you haven't filed a claim for auto or home insurance in the past seven years, or a Resident Data if you haven't been a tenant. There may be a fraudulent report for you, however, if claims were made by your impostor.

Instead of ordering separate reports, you can order the complete ChoicePoint file on you. It not only includes all the information from the three different reports, but it adds information available on you in public records, including the following:

- ◆ Real-estate transactions and ownership
- ◆ Lien, judgment, and bankruptcy
- ◆ Professional licenses
- ◆ History of personal addresses
- ◆ Summaries of historic auto or homeowner insurance coverage
- ◆ Pre-employment background check, if one was done
- ◆ National criminal records check

There is a separate form and set of instructions on the site to get this information. ChoicePoint only mails it. You can get the complete report free once a year. The site also has instructions about how to challenge any information in the file.

Special Cases

Two areas—employment and insurance—require slightly different treatment than the financial fraud in this chapter.

Employment Fraud

Employment identity theft is usually invisible. The fraudster uses your Social Security number (maybe with someone else's name) to earn wages. This causes the IRS to question and possibly audit your true tax return. Your impostor may have filed a tax return before you filed one for a given year and received a refund. You may be investigated and a tax lien may appear on your credit report. If your impostor takes money out of a 401(k) plan, pension, Social Security, or disability insurance and has used your Social Security number, the IRS may also have questions because the money may be taxable.

Even worse, your impostor might be planning to embezzle money, facilitate money laundering, or commit other crimes while working veiled under your identity. No matter what the situation, you'll need to probe the facts to avoid financial loss or criminal prosecution.

Not all employers run a credit check before hiring someone, so you cannot be sure that no one is working under your name just by reviewing the information on your credit report. Credit reports from the CRAs will list employment history in your personal information, so examine this section and call any employer you don't recognize. If the employer states that a person with your Social Security number did work for the company, you'll have to get all documentation of the employment using the letter format recommended in this chapter. If an impostor is using your Social Security number (whether or not he uses your name), eventually the IRS will catch up with you—perhaps years later.

If you find that an employer hired your impersonator, find out what benefits the person received. Make sure you also inform law enforcement in the city of the impostor. You may also have a legal cause of action against the employer (see Chapter 18). If you experience problems with health insurance as a result of your impostor's receiving employee benefits, proceed to Chapter 14.

Information = Power

Once you obtain original applications from creditors and others, carefully read them. The application will list an employer. That may give you a warning of employment identity fraud. Often, however, the impostor will not give the name of a real employer. Impersonators will often give a name and phone number of a co-conspirator to verify employment.

Because the information on credit reports may be incomplete, get your ChoicePoint employment history report for details.

Insurance Fraud

Insurance fraud by an identity thief is even trickier to catch than employment fraud because the insurance companies don't always do a credit check. Furthermore, if a carrier doesn't get paid, it doesn't even need to use a collection agency. The company simply cancels the coverage, losing nothing. You may think it's not a problem that will affect you, but think again.

It can be insidious and potentially dangerous. A client of mine once learned that a fraudster took out a life-insurance policy in her name, naming himself as the beneficiary. She only found out about the sham when she herself tried to get her own life-insurance policy. Finding and ending the charade may have saved her life when the impostor was sent to jail. Another client found that his impostor obtained business insurance in his name and was later sued for malpractice.

Your impostor sets up an insurance policy to protect a home, car, his health, or disability, so the insurance may be linked to an asset that was purchased or leased in your name. If an auto accident occurs, you could be sued or even lose your license. If someone gets hurt at the home, you could be sued. If the fraudster files for disability and the carriers find that you are still working, you could be prosecuted for fraud. Criminals may file fraudulent claims and make it look as though you were at fault. As with employment fraud, don't make the mistake of dismissing any suspicious letters or notices about insurance issues.

To clear the problem, you will need to deal with various commercial and governmental entities. As with employment fraud, head to www. ChoicePoint.com. In this case, though, don't be satisfied with the C.L.U.E. report, which only covers claims history. Be sure to get the full ChoicePoint file on you, which has not only claims but also your public records, so you will find out about properties owned in your name, professional licenses, and more that might give clues into insurance the fraudster has taken out.

To challenge information in your ChoicePoint report, use the procedures you used under your FCRA rights to dispute fraud with the credit reporting agencies.

Information brokers like ChoicePoint are also considered specialty consumer reporting entities under FCRA, so you have a right to a free annual report, a right to review, dispute, and correct such reports. Write your letter disputing the fraud and clarifying the errors. Attach your identity-theft report and affidavit, and send, return receipt requested.

Information = Power

If you are concerned that your identity may be used for financial purposes that are not revealed on your credit reports, you may use a free service at www.myidscore.com to determine your risk of identity theft. Using such identity elements as name, Social Security number, phone number, date of birth, and address, My ID Score calculates a statistical score. The higher the score, the greater the risk that you may be a victim of fraud that may not be immediately evident to you.

The Least You Need to Know

◆ Not all financial fraud accounts will show up on your credit reports.

◆ Look at the inquiries section of your credit reports to find suspicious companies to investigate.

- ◆ Order your free non-credit consumer reports from ChoicePoint and NCTUE.

- ◆ Employment ID theft may indicate other types of financial and insurance fraud.

Part 3

The Innocent and Betrayals

Not everyone has the ability to deal with his or her own identity-theft problems. Children, elderly, the ill, and the dearly departed are often targets of identity-theft vultures because none of them have the power to discover or challenge the fraud themselves, which is why you are there to help!

Each presents different challenges, although they are similar in the sense that *you* must assert *their* legal rights. It can take years for child identity theft to come to light. For those who have passed on, not only is reputation at stake, but usually the estate and heirs become victims.

A heartbreaking challenge arises when someone close to you—friend or relative—has stolen your identity, because you may not want to prosecute. I'll show you potential alternatives to the normal step of getting law enforcement involved, so that you can recover without jail time for someone you care about.

Chapter 9

Child Identity Theft

In This Chapter

- ◆ Why children are easy targets
- ◆ Verifying that a child's identity was stolen
- ◆ Modifying identity restoration for a child
- ◆ When to hire a lawyer
- ◆ Helping children deal with their feelings

An identity thief is despicable, stealing goods and services and leaving you to blame. What's even more appalling is when fraudsters steal the identity of a child. These criminals may leave the children with identity mayhem that can last a long time because the signs of theft may not show up for years. If you have a strong suspicion that someone has stolen your child's identity, this chapter will show you the steps necessary to recover it.

Sadly, child identity theft is often perpetrated by someone who is or was close to the family: an estranged parent, former stepparent, family friend, or an insider from a company or office that you and your child frequent. Under some circumstances you may want to make the thief accountable without law-enforcement intervention, for the sake of the family. In that case, see Chapter 11 for details of how to proceed. But if the time has come to burn bridges and help prosecute, this is the chapter to use.

Children Are Prime Targets

When a stranger steals your child's identity, it's for one reason: convenient financial benefit. Someone who is under 16 probably has no work history and no credit profile at all. Parents or guardians may have set up a bank or college account, but that won't appear on a credit report. Young people offer thieves the opportunity to go undercover to work, obtain credit, and even avoid prosecution for other crimes.

Some identity thieves steal goods, services, loans, credit lines, open new bank accounts, and even create criminal records. This leaves a path of destruction that waits for the child to grow old enough to apply for a job, buy a car, or rent an apartment. Other fraudsters may be illegally in our country, needing a Social Security number to work, and so using a child's identity for employment. Or someone might use a child's Social Security number to get a driver's license after his or her own has been suspended. Upon arrest, some criminals give the stolen Social Security number and name, meaning your child could have a criminal record before he or she even starts school.

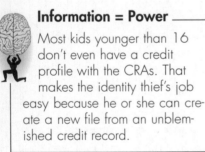

Information = Power

Most kids younger than 16 don't even have a credit profile with the CRAs. That makes the identity thief's job easy because he or she can create a new file from an unblemished credit record.

To put it bluntly, child identity theft is serious, and can be worse because the ramifications will often not be revealed until he or she becomes an unsuspecting young adult. I saw the case of one young man denied a driver's license, student loans, and employment because an estranged stepfather ruined his identity. It took years to straighten out, and he'll still need to monitor his credit reports and perform criminal background checks for the rest of his life.

How Could It Happen?

You might be wondering how babies could have their identities stolen. Often newborns receive a Social Security number while at the hospital. A rogue healthcare employee or unauthorized access of medical data can be enough to make this key to the kingdom of identity theft available to a fraudster.

In our society of automation and vast databases, creditors simply haven't verified or authenticated applicants for credit. They have regularly granted credit without even asking for proof of identity. Staff may be badly trained or a company may decide that the cost savings of avoiding the time and effort to perform proper checks outweighs the cost of fraud when found and contested. Profit from most non-fraud accounts is outweighed by the fraud, and it takes time and effort to do due diligence.

The CRAs have not independently verified personal information, including age or date of birth. As the child does not have a credit record prior to the fraudster's activity, whatever is reported as a date of birth by the creditor, which is the date provided by the fraudster, becomes what the CRA believes is correct, until proven otherwise.

Red Flag Rules

Some new Red Flag Rules under FCRA require companies that extend credit to implement an identity-theft prevention plan, which will hopefully help remedy some of the problem.

Each financial institution or creditor with any consumer accounts, or other accounts for which there is a reasonably foreseeable risk of identity theft, must develop and implement an Identity Theft Prevention Program. The program must include reasonable policies and procedures to detect, prevent, and mitigate identity theft. The financial institution or creditor must be able to:

1. Identify activities that are "red flags" for possible identity theft.

2. Detect the red flags through in-house investigation.

3. Respond appropriately to any red flags that are detected to prevent and mitigate identity theft.

4. Ensure the program is periodically updated to reflect changes in risks from identity theft.

For you or your child as a victim, you will focus on number 3 above to make sure that the company mitigates the effects of identity theft and resolve the issues quickly.

Signs of Child ID Theft

If you're reading this chapter, then you're concerned that someone has stolen your child's identity. The warning signs will be similar to that of adults. Your child may receive any of the following, either while still young or after becoming an adult:

◆ Collection-agency calls.

◆ Bills or pre-approved credit card offers sent to your home.

◆ IRS letters demanding payment.

◆ Law enforcement notices or warnings.

◆ Denial of a driver's license, student loans, credit cards, or insurance.

◆ Someone with access to your child's SSN and other information either suddenly has money, is able to get a driver's license when the old one was revoked or suspended, is able to get credit cards, or exhibits other unexplained reversal in fortunes.

◆ Notices about traffic violations, back taxes owed, or liens.

◆ A government program denies benefits because the child is already getting them.

Information = Power

Don't panic. Children with savings or college accounts in their names often receive pre-approved credit-card offers because an automated system identified the child as creditworthy. Immediately call 1-888-5-OPT-OUT to opt out of having your child's name and identity sold on promotion.

All of these are warning signs to take immediate action. When your child becomes a young adult and has difficulties getting credit or a job and there is no reasonable explanation for the challenges, it's time to immediately investigate. Treat the situation as identity fraud.

Tricks of Child Identity Recovery

If your child is at least 18 and has just discovered problems from identity theft from earlier years, then he or she must take the recovery approach to identity starting with Chapter 2 through Chapter 4, and moving on as necessary to appropriate steps in other chapters.

Most recovery steps are the same for minor children; however, you'll be calling and writing on behalf of your child and must provide additional proof of your identity. For every business or entity affected by the fraud, you must include the following, in addition to everything else mentioned in Chapters 2 through 4:

- Child's full name

- Child's Social Security number

- Child's addresses for the last five years

- Child's date of birth

- Copies of the child's birth certificate and Social Security card

- Copies of the child's school records for the past five years

- Your name and address

- Proof of your relation to the child (should be on the birth certificate or adoption or guardian documents)

- That you are requesting information on your child's behalf as the parent and legal guardian

- You are requesting all documents of the fraud associated with your child's SSN pursuant to FCRA 609(e)

As always, the first step is to contact all three CRAs by phone and place a fraud alert on your child's profile. The fraudster has already established an address, so you may not be able to set the alert by phone. If that is the case, immediately send a letter informing the CRAs of the fraud and requesting a copy of the report if there is one. Explain that you are investigating a case of child identity theft. Ask the bureaus to place a security freeze on your child's credit profile and provide you with a password to use to "thaw the file" when your child is old enough for a report to be established.

Identity Crisis

TransUnion says that it has a special e-mail address to which you can send a child's name and Social Security number to get a Yes or No answer whether there is a credit record. *Do not use it!* You would be sending that sensitive information unprotected where it could possibly be intercepted and misused. Instead, always send letters return receipt requested to the credit bureaus so you will have a receipt of the correspondence.

In your letter (as always, sent return receipt requested), provide the evidence that someone stole your child's identity. You will get one of two possible answers. If the response is that the CRA has no credit record for the child, there could be other types of fraud not appearing on reports. Refer to Chapters 7 and 8.

If your child has a record, then you must get the credit reports and dispute them. If you change your child's Social Security number (more on that later in this chapter), you must write the bureaus and ask that they not only remove the fraud, but take the profile offline because your child has a new Social Security number. To remove the fraud from the child's credit profile, you, as the parent, must complete the steps in Chapters 5 and 6 on your child's behalf.

Information = Power

Whenever disputing credit accounts, purchases, or other forms of financial fraud, be sure to note that the child is a minor and cannot enter into a legal and binding contract, and that you, as parent or legal guardian, have the right to remove all fraud. Provide your own Social Security number and identifying documents to the creditors as well.

Depending on what made you think there was a case of identity theft, you may need to continue your investigation:

♦ If someone seems to have obtained a driver's license or other government-issued ID in the child's name, Chapter 12 will give details of how to handle the problem.

♦ If there is a question of a problem with the child's medical records, then go to Chapter 14.

♦ If you've received a court notice for criminal action, go to Chapter 15.

♦ If someone is taking civil action against the child, see Chapter 16.

Children and Social Security Numbers

I always advise adult victims of identity theft never to seek a new Social Security number from the government. You look suspicious, because the new Social Security number will pull up and link to the old one through myriad databases. Even with an explanation of identity theft, companies and agencies will raise questions about your character. It's better for adults to keep their Social Security numbers and make corrections to their existing records.

For a child of 16 years or younger, the situation is different. Kids haven't established their own credit yet. You can change the child's Social Security number without too much worry about the multitude of databases identifying his name with that number (unless you have established several accounts in his name). It's also a way to keep further activity by the fraudster from coming back to harm your child. See Chapter 12 for details on obtaining a new Social Security number.

When to Involve a Lawyer

Except in extreme cases, you don't need a lawyer to recover your identity or resolve your child's identity. But in some circumstances you may find that a lawyer is necessary.

For example, it may be that an ex-spouse or stepparent is the identity thief. The action may become part of divorce or custody proceedings. If the thief is a relative, law-enforcement officials may not want to provide a report because they might consider it a civil action and, if there is a divorce, they will encourage you to address the issues with your family-law attorney. If your child's identity was stolen by someone who committed felonies, there will be criminal prosecution or convictions, and you will need to take defensive action with the courts. At such times, find a qualified attorney who understands both identity theft and the other legal issues involved. (See Chapter 18.)

Handling the Emotional Hurt

It is hard enough for adults to deal with cases of stolen identity and the feelings of anguish, violation, and rage that will come up. But a young adult who finds out as a teenager that a criminal has done this will be far less equipped to manage the overwhelming emotional challenges and frustration, especially if the criminal was a family member. Children may blame themselves for the situation, believing they must have done something wrong and that they are being punished for their actions. They may also live in fear if they never find out who did this to them—statistics show that only about 12 percent of victims find out who perpetrated the crime.

Help the child understand that the person who committed the acts did so for his or her financial benefit, and that the child had nothing to do with it, did nothing wrong, and couldn't have prevented it. Ease the child's fears by noting that most identity thieves will never physically harm the victim, because money is their target. It's unlikely that the child will ever meet the impostor, unless the criminal is a family member. If that's the case, consider counseling and spiritual guidance for the child, so he or she can learn how to handle the fear, anger, and betrayal.

The Least You Need to Know

- Receiving a pre-approved offer in the mail doesn't necessarily mean that someone stole your child's identity.

- Point out to any creditors that your child is a minor and could not enter a contract.

◆ Send proof of your child's identity and age along with the usual other material in correspondence.

◆ If a relative was involved, read Chapter 11 for additional considerations.

◆ If there are custody, divorce, or criminal issues, consult a lawyer.

◆ If your child is old enough to understand the identity theft, consider counseling for the emotional issues.

Chapter 10

Even the Deceased Can Be Victims

In This Chapter

- ◆ Determining whether a deceased loved one is an identity-theft victim

- ◆ Managing the unique problems of reclaiming the identity of someone who has died

- ◆ Recovering the identity of the departed

When it comes to money, there's an old saying: You can't take it with you. And if you are a deceased victim of identity theft, you can't take your good name and reputation, either. Identity thieves find that impersonating someone who has died allows them to undertake their criminal behavior more easily, because the victim is no longer using his or her own identity and in some cases no one will notice a problem or take action to stop it.

But the pain, cost, and time incurred by the surviving loved ones is tremendous. Not only is there the emotional loss of a dear one's passing, but having to clean up the fraud and deal with companies trying to lay claim to the person's estate is overwhelming, especially for a widowed spouse.

Knowing the Deceased Is Targeted

Like other types of identity fraud, you'll learn that your late loved one is a victim when collection phone calls and letters arrive for the deceased months after his or her passing. When you obtain billing statements and other documents, it's common that the charges and actions took place after your loved one died.

In the most heartbreaking scenario, a parent who has lost a child may hear from a company or even government authority asking for the child's whereabouts. Fraudsters can learn a lot about a person who has died from obituaries in the newspaper and family trees at genealogy sites on the Internet. (In fact, it's a good idea not to post family trees online because they provide fraudsters with good information for stealing an identity.) It's easy for an impostor to use a deceased person's good name and reputation to work, get credit, obtain government benefits, avoid prosecution, or do anything that the live person could have done.

Information = Power _____

Impersonation of deceased children has become very common since infants have received Social Security numbers shortly after birth, as Chapter 9 describes. Famous hacker turned security expert Kevin Mitnick told me on my radio show that he used names and Social Security numbers of deceased children when hiding from authorities so he could work and live undetected. When he thought authorities were near, he'd move to another town, look up death records, and steal the identity of another child. Although he said he always paid the bills, imagine the shock when parents received mailings in the dead child's name.

Unfortunately, getting personal information for someone who recently died is often no more difficult than going to the U.S. Death Index or looking through the newspaper obituaries and copying the mass of biographical detail listed as part of a commemoration or getting a copy of the U.S. Social Security Death Index. (The SSDI is an easily obtained, regularly updated list of people that the Social Security Administration lists as having died. It includes the person's Social Security number.)

If the deceased is a good target (in other words, appears wealthy), the fraudster may go online and start the fraud. And because the Social Security Administration is often very slow in reporting deaths to CRAs—and family members forget to report the death to the SSA—the identity thief may have ample opportunity to obtain credit in the deceased's name.

The first step is to contact the credit bureaus and order copies of the deceased's credit reports. Dealing with the deceased's identity theft presents some special challenges.

Unique Problems

The main problem facing the victim's relatives is convincing law enforcement, CRAs, creditors, and others to believe that the family representative has the authority to take action on the deceased's behalf. It will be less difficult for a surviving spouse because the credit report lists the spouse's name and other information that shows similarity, such as name, address, and phone number.

You will need to first provide your evidence of the right to dispute the fraud. Once you have the authority to step into your loved one's shoes, you will follow the steps in Chapters 2 through 5 and others as necessary.

Information = Power

Although it is frustrating when entities make it difficult for you to clear your loved one's good name, consider that the entities themselves have been defrauded. So as a surviving heir, it's your job to prove that there was fraud and that you had nothing to do with it.

Here's what you will need to add to letters to CRAs, creditors, and other entities, in addition to other previously explained information and material, to establish your right to dispute the fraud:

- Certificate of death for the departed

- A statement indicating why you believe the deceased is a victim of identity theft

- Proof corroborating your relationship to the deceased

- Proof that you have the authority to act for the estate

Depending on the circumstances, proof of relationship may be easy. There may be evidence in a will, trust, beneficiary funds document, life insurance, joint bank accounts, or other beneficiary or court document. If the deceased was your spouse, then a copy of a marriage certificate, a copy of your driver's license, a copy of the personal information section on your own credit report, a will or trust document, a copy of a utility bill or bank statement showing that you live at the same address as the deceased will help. An adult child of the victim may use a birth certificate that would list the deceased as a parent, along with documents showing a maiden name for a daughter.

If you're a more distant relative, showing proof may be more difficult. One client of mine was the niece of an uncle who died without children, and showing a direct relationship was virtually impossible, as she didn't have the paper trail of a will or trust that a direct descendent would have. As the sole surviving heir, she had to make the funeral arrangements, so she pulled together all documents demonstrating that she was responsible for the estate and funeral arrangements after her uncle's death. The CRAs and creditors finally accepted her evidence and allowed her access to documents to resolve the fraud.

Information = Power

If you don't have documents to show you are an executor or trustee, have power of attorney, or are a direct descendant, then you must show how you are acting in the deceased's best interest by presenting documents and letters regarding your actions. For my client whose uncle died, her own affidavit, a bank guarantee of her signature, and demonstration of the actions she took for the funeral were sufficient for the CRA's creditors and governmental agencies to believe her.

Proving Authority

Under the law, only a person who can represent the deceased's estate has the authority to get the records and demand the changes necessary to recover the identity. Typically that means one of the following:

- A direct heir

- Someone who had power-of-attorney for the person before death

- The attorney in fact for the estate

- The executor of the person's will

- A trustee of a trust in the deceased's name

If you can show you're the child or spouse of the deceased, that will generally satisfy the requirement. If you are the closest living relative, you will be best served by any documents you can find that may be filed with the court or found in public records that show the connection. For example, if needed, my client whose uncle died could have obtained his birth certificate as well as the birth certificate of her mother, who was the uncle's sister, to show a family connection. Then she could have included her own birth certificate as proof of the family relation. Consider all the proof you have and send copies of it along with your letter, affidavit, and police report.

Identity Crisis

If there is a will or trust, you need to send copies of relevant pages that show you are the executor, trustee, or heir of the estate.

Once you provide documents to prove your relationship to the deceased and your authority to act on his or her behalf, you'll be ready to take the necessary steps to restore your loved one's good name.

Clearing the Name and Protecting the Estate

Although many of the steps are going to be similar to recovering one's own identify, there are additional tasks to perform. Here's the procedure to use, and the order in which you need to act:

1. Call the Social Security Administration at 1-800-772-1213 and notify them of your loved one's passing. Follow up with a letter sent certified return receipt requested.

2. Contact the CRAs by phone to place a fraud alert on the person's file. You will not speak to a live person. Provide the Social Security number and address and you'll get a letter from each of the three CRAs entitling you to write them for a free credit report.

3. Determine which accounts are fraudulent by comparing them to the accounts that are genuine. Determining which is which may be a feat in itself. Look for fraudulent addresses on the report, the date the accounts were opened, the dates of inquiries, and accounts that are in arrears.

4. Get a law-enforcement identity-theft report, as explained in Chapter 2. You will need to show the death certificate and some evidence of the fraud to get the report.

5. Fill out the identity-theft victim affidavit, explicitly stating that the victim is deceased and you are acting as the representative of the victim's estate.

6. Write the CRAs to dispute the accounts and inquiries. Include a copy of the death certificate, an affidavit, a copy of your loved one's utility statement, evidence of your relation, and a copy of the law-enforcement report. Inform the CRAs that the person has died and that they should immediately place a "deceased alert" on the credit file and take the file offline so no other creditor can access it. Also demand that they immediately inform all third parties that have requested copies of the credit profile.

7. If you have not already done so, contact all true creditors and business relationships of the deceased. Ask them to close accounts or, if there are bank accounts or investments that are part of the estate, provide a power of attorney and other documents to manage the estate so that you may also protect those accounts and transfer funds to new account numbers with new passwords. If your late spouse was a victim, close joint accounts and transfer any money to new accounts.

8. Contact all creditors and other third parties that have either created fraudulent accounts or have requested a credit report after the

person died. In each case, explain the identity theft and establish the timing of the death. Be sure to include a copy of the death certificate. This will establish that the deceased could not have been responsible for the charges on the account. If crimes were committed by the impostor after the person's death, you will establish death as the perfect alibi.

9. Notify the Internal Revenue Service about the fraud. You will need to fill out an estate tax return for the deceased. Let the IRS know about the fraud before they notify you of underpayment if a fraudster used the deceased's Social Security number to work or to obtain other financial benefits. See Chapter 12 for more information.

10. If the deceased was on Medicare or Medicaid or had private health insurance, or received Social Security payments or retirement income, contact the agency or insurance company and report the death to stop someone else from claiming those benefits. Look at Chapter 14 for details on handling medical identity theft and clearing records with Medicare, Medicaid, or other health carriers.

Information = Power _____

The IRS has instructions on how to file a return for someone who has died. Go to www.irs.gov and download Publication 559, "Survivor, Executors, and Administrators," for details on what to do.

11. If the deceased had a professional license, contact that state's licensing authority and inform it that the person has died, and to place an alert in the file so an impostor doesn't use the license. Chapter 12 has details for dealing with professional licenses.

If an attorney is involved in the resolution of the estate, understand that probate is distinct from identity theft and you may need to educate the attorney about the fraud issues. If the case must go through probate, the courts must also be notified of the fraud.

If you are having trouble getting entities to allow you to be the representative to restore the estate and your loved one's good name, your family's estate attorney can vouch for your identity and relationship to the deceased and can write a letter on your behalf.

Contact ChoicePoint (www.choicepoint.com) to get a background check to see if the impostor committed crimes. Notify ChoicePoint of the death of your loved one, and ask that a deceased alert be added to information regarding the name of the departed.

The Least You Need to Know

♦ Get proof of your relationship to the deceased and your authority to act for his or her estate before you attempt resolution.

♦ Inform the Social Security Administration, the IRS, Medicare, Medicaid, your state's Department of Motor Vehicles, and any other relevant government agencies, financial institutions, and other relevant entities of the death of your loved one.

♦ Contact all companies that your loved one did business with and ask them to appropriately update, transfer, or close the accounts.

♦ Contact the CRAs to inform them of the death and the fraud, and ask them to take the deceased's profile offline.

♦ Contact all entities involved in the fraudulent activity and ask them to remove any fraudulent entry from their records and to notify third parties who obtained such records.

Chapter 11

Family and Friend Fakes

In This Chapter

- ◆ Why friends and family steal identities
- ◆ How identity recovery differs when the thief is known to you rather than a stranger
- ◆ Alternative approaches to identity restoration
- ◆ Dealing with identity theft by a spouse or ex-spouse

An FTC study in 2006 found that about 12 percent of identity theft is committed by a family member or friend. The fraudster may have been a child, parent, stepparent, best friend, confidant, or even a present or former spouse.

It's a devastating situation. On one hand, the victim feels betrayed, psychologically and financially violated. On the other hand, the victim may still feel sentimental ties to the family member, and may be reluctant to get the important law-enforcement report. Family and friends may try to intercede on behalf of the person who wronged you, to protect him or her from prosecution or legal action by companies who were defrauded. If the thief is a co-worker, your supervisor might want the incident covered up, so as not to bring bad publicity to the company.

This chapter focuses on how to deal effectively with circumstances in which you may feel ambivalent. I'll show you how to protect yourself, hold the revealed impostor accountable, and handle this difficult situation effectively.

When Family Members and Friends Steal

If a family member steals your identity, it's usually for money, purchases, services, or, unfortunately, even to avoid arrest. Someone who knows you well can have lots of sensitive, personal information about you, including your birth date, SSN, and extensive knowledge about your life. It's so easy to steal the identity of someone you know.

Identity Crisis

If a spouse has stolen your identity, unless you are separated and have filed a police report, it is unlikely that you will be considered a victim of fraud. Marital-property laws protect companies collecting debts incurred by spouses. If, however, you are going through a divorce, fraud must be addressed in the dissolution case so that a court may rule on the issue of the debts. If you settle through negotiation, your Marital Settlement Agreement must delineate which spouse will assume which debts, and how you will indemnify each other if a creditor goes after the wrong spouse.

The theft of your identity by a friend or family member is a betrayal of your trust. It's important to remember that you did nothing to warrant your family member or friend's robbery of your identity. Don't feel guilty for wanting that impostor to take responsibility for his or her actions. You do have a right to be hurt, angry, and frustrated. You may even be incredulous that the person would do this to you. But people with personality disorders are capable of doing things to benefit themselves with complete disregard for anyone else's welfare, and no remorse.

Most often, a person who steals the identity of a friend or relative is someone in a financial bind. The thief could be addicted to alcohol or drugs (methamphetamine and identity theft are closely linked in a huge number of prosecuted cases) and needs money for the next fix. I've had clients betrayed by stepsiblings, parents, and children. Your impostor may be greedy, have a financial hardship, or another reason, but there is no good excuse for committing this crime.

Hidden Agenda

Identity theft by someone the victim knows is not the most common type; however, it is the most devastating. According to Federal Trade Commission statistics, six percent of victims are related to the fraudster. Approximately six percent of the time the criminal is a friend, neighbor, a business associate, or someone who works at the victim's home. Two percent of the time, the person is a co-worker. That's a whopping 16 percent of identity-theft cases. On the other hand, 84 percent of cases are committed by a stranger, and only about 10 percent of the time will you even find out who that person is. It is unlikely that your impostor will ever be arrested.

Many identity thieves who are close to their victims try to rationalize what they did. They convince themselves that they are not bad people and that there should be no serious consequences for them. I hope you don't fall for this line of reasoning.

When someone close to you has stolen your identity, he or she has taken advantage of you because your sensitive information was readily available and easy to use. Although the person may claim every intention of paying you back or that it was just borrowing from you, now you face the challenge of dealing with myriad companies and governmental agencies to restore your good reputation. You need to clear up the issues; however, it can be more difficult than when a stranger steals your identity.

Challenges of Familiar ID Theft

The close relationship you have with the fraudster can also make you look like the co-conspirator, defrauding companies issuing credit. Creditors are skeptical when a family member is the thief. The in-house fraud investigators often assume that if a relative is involved, there may be collusion or even an attempt by one family member to unjustly blame the other.

When a relative or friend is involved, law enforcement will often try to tag the identity theft as a domestic dispute or a civil action, and will try to avoid giving you a report, even though it's clearly a criminal matter under federal and state law. So unfortunately you have extra barriers to proving your innocence, but once you understand them, you can overcome them.

Remember that there are three basic actions necessary to successfully regain your identity:

1. You report the crime to a local, state, or federal law-enforcement agency so that you may obtain an identity-theft report to send to all agencies as proof of your innocence.

2. You provide your completed FTC affidavit explaining what you know about the fraud.

3. You cooperate with the creditor's in-house investigators and others by being honest about the facts of the fraud.

When you know the thief, any or all of these actions may be very complicated. You may feel uncomfortable reporting the person to law enforcement (especially if your child or parent is the perpetrator) because you fear that person will go to jail, leaving you feeing responsible and guilty. The reality is that only about 10 percent of identity-theft cases are investigated by law enforcement, and once they know it is family, they usually won't take the case and file charges. That doesn't guarantee that the defrauded company won't press charges, but they usually don't. It takes a great deal of time and it's unlikely that the fraudster has the money to pay restitution, so it's not worth it to the companies.

Identity Crisis

Pretending that you don't know the identity thief is dangerous and fraudulent. Trying to cover for the impostor would require you to commit a felony. In addition, you destroy trust with both law enforcement and creditors, and will be seen as a co-conspirator.

You may also find yourself pressured by family members or friends of the thief, urging you to "be nice." If the thief is a co-worker, your supervisor might want the incident covered up, so as not to bring bad publicity to the company. Relatives may offer to help "fix" the problem if you agree not to go to the police. Now you are facing internal conflict, ambivalence, and alienation if you do what you need to do to regain your life, but don't despair.

Handling Familiar ID Theft

The emotional toll of family or friend identity theft is incalculable. When you have been betrayed by someone close to you, you feel you cannot trust anymore. You feel torn inside as you debate what's fair to you and what others may tell you to do to protect the fraudster. It may help to know that you have some choices in how to handle the identity theft. These are as follows:

♦ If the family member is estranged or if the impostor was a former friend, then treat the identity theft as you would a stranger, including reporting to the authorities, no matter what the consequences for the thief. In most cases of identity theft, the victim has no idea who the thief is, but in your case, you have caught the impostor "red-handed."

♦ Get the thief to accept responsibility and convince the creditors to transfer the debt to the impostor's Social Security number, so that he is accountable and your name is cleared. They may not want to do that because the fraudster's credit is probably poor. If they ask you to pay it for them, or they pay through you, it still remains on your credit report.

♦ Although I never recommend this option, some victims who called had gritted their teeth and assumed the debt as though it were their own. Although angry, some victims accepted the long-term financial and emotional consequences. At that point, when victims call me upset at what they have done, I cannot help them and can only suggest counseling about their issue of co-dependence.

The choice of how you deal with the family perpetrator will depend on the circumstances; what is most important to you; and if the identity thief finally is willing to act honorably as well as admit the misuse of your identity. If the thief is a present or former spouse, then look at the section at the end of this chapter.

Identity Crisis

If you wish to help the family member to be responsible and also take care of yourself, you have some options. But I recommend that under no circumstances should you pay any of the family fraudster's bills in your name. Some victims have worked out a signed agreement with the family perpetrator for repayment. But I don't believe that is an acceptable solution. Once you pay any of the money owed to creditors in your name, you've accepted responsibility for the charges and bills as though they were your own, and those accounts will appear on your credit reports for seven years if you don't dispute them as fraud. If your impostor has filed for bankruptcy in your name, it will be on your reports for 10 years and your financial reputation is ruined. So no matter how close you are to the perpetrator, don't let yourself be abused.

Take No Prisoners

The title of this section is tough, but I feel strongly that an identity thief who is an estranged family fraudster or now-former friend should be treated like the criminal he truly is. What the thief did was wrong and was done without consideration of your reputation or your finances. Perhaps worse, it may have given you a criminal record. This firm approach is not painless. The fraudster's family and friends will try to get you to be merciful. But if the person you know committed this crime and gets away with it, he or she will probably do it to someone else. You should not feel guilty taking all measures to restore your identity.

Keep a few other things in mind, too. Even if you make a report to law enforcement, chances are that the police will not investigate or arrest the identity thief, particularly if he or she is a relative. It will be a challenge even getting an identity-theft report. If law enforcement does decide to investigate, prosecution becomes even less likely because the district attorney's office and federal prosecutors have much bigger cases, unless your impostor defrauded other victims.

To escape from the nightmare of identity theft, you must be diligent. To refuse to work with police or in-house investigators of defrauded companies will make you look guilty in the eyes of others. If law enforcement won't take a report, you'll look guilty to the creditors.

Push to get at least an informational report, as Chapter 2 explains. Any time a creditor asks whether you will be willing to prosecute a relative or friend, answer as follows: "I am cooperating fully with law enforcement. I have no control over whether law enforcement investigates or arrests the person, nor whether the district attorney will prosecute."

You may remind the creditor that it is a victim and should make its own police report as well. Do not be intimated by in-house credit investigators; the creditor is just looking for an excuse to make you pay the money stolen by the impostor. Be polite, but be firm. If a company tries to tell you that you will have to pay if your family impostor will not, tell them that it is not the law and not true because you are a victim under FCRA and they cannot make you pay for authorized purchases.

Information = Power

If local police will not issue a report, tell them that the Fair Credit Reporting Act requires that you get a report to regain your identity. If that doesn't work, remember that you have alternatives to obtain an identity-theft report. If the thief used the mail (for example, had credit cards delivered by mail), you may call your local Postal Inspector. If your Social Security number was used, call your local office of the Social Security Administration (Chapter 2).

Bargaining with Creditors

If your guilt, or the thief's pleading, or your family members' disapproval is too unbearable, there is an alternative. If the impostor is willing to be accountable and honest and accept the debt as his or her own, this approach should suffice. Tell your impostor that if he or she is honest and takes responsibility, then that should be enough for you to clear your name. On the other hand, let him or her know that if he or she does not deal with the creditor, then you must get an identity-theft report according to FCRA requirements for you to clear your name with the CRAs and the creditors. You will be forced to protect yourself any way you can. The fraudster's admission to the creditors along with a promise to pay will help to get the creditors to remove the accounts from your credit files. This is not extortion; it is explaining the consequences.

The identity thief must voluntarily sign a notarized affidavit accepting responsibility for the debt, and explain that you did not authorize the use of your Social Security number and you received no benefit. He or she must provide a copy of a government-issued ID, a utility statement, and a copy of the affidavit explaining what he or she did (and why, if it's a sad story).

The impostor must give his or her Social Security number, agree to assume all responsibility for the debt, provide all his contact information, and ask the creditor or agency to communicate with him. Make sure your impostor gives you a copy of all the documentation above for you also to send along with copies of your FTC affidavit and government-issued ID. You must send this to the fraud department return receipt requested. You will send this letter to the creditor and any other entity involved in the scam, as well as the CRAs telling them of the fraud. Demand that your credit be cleared and the real culprit be held responsible.

You are asking the creditors to accept that the thief, not you, is responsible for the fraud. It is a deal between the creditors and the thief, not between you and the thief. The creditor would have to agree to no longer coming after you with this evidence of fraud and, instead, transfer the debt from you to the thief. This may sound like a fine solution, but it has some thorny problems:

♦ Without filing a complaint with law enforcement and getting an identity-theft victim report, you may be denied your legal rights under FCRA.

♦ Federal law does not obligate creditors to accept an admission from the identity thief. If the thief has no money, the creditors will be reluctant to transfer the debt. So they may tell you they can't do anything without a police report. I suggest you get the police report and show the police the fraudster's affidavit. Since the impostor is willing to take responsibility, it is very unlikely that law enforcement will refer the case further, even if the creditor files its own police report. In essence, the fraudster is agreeing to make restitution to the company.

♦ Creditors may be suspicious of a friend or relative claiming responsibility for what another seems to owe, which is why he must say that you did not authorize the use of your credit and received nothing.

♦ Creditors have a disincentive to let you off the hook if they believe they're more likely to get money from you than from someone who's broke and has already committed fraud.

♦ Once an entity accepts the fraud claim, even if the thief stops paying, the creditors cannot legally come back to get the money from you. Once the account is deleted from your credit report due to fraud, under FCRA the creditors cannot re-report the account on your credit profile.

♦ Creditors cannot demand the entire owed amount be paid before they release you from responsibility if you have proven the fraud. So if your impostor doesn't pay all agreed installment payments, the company can only go after him or her.

Identity Crisis

If the identity thief is unwilling to accept formal responsibility and sign a notarized affidavit admitting the fraud and assuming the debt, then the approach above will not work. If the impostor won't be honest and take responsibility, tell him that you are forced to protect yourself and will file a police report, telling law enforcement and the companies what you know, and proceed to restore your good name as though you didn't know the thief.

Giving In to Guilt

If the fraudster is your own son or daughter, or mother or father, you may experience enormous pain and guilt even if the impostor refuses to take responsibility. To me, paying the impostor's bills and ruining your financial life and hard-earned reputation is not acceptable. It teaches the family member that crime pays, and it leaves you saddled with the credit stigma for the next seven years or more.

Even if family or friends beg you not to hold the thief accountable, and they are willing to pay all of the debt, remember that the negative marks on your credit report won't go away just because the debts are paid. There may be numerous late payment and collection accounts. If family members are willing to pay for the fraudster, work out an agreement with the company and the family members.

Encourage the family members to also pay for a lawyer to work out an agreement with the company, the fraudster, and you regarding the payoff. I suggest that the family members get all the money to pay off the fraudulent debts at the time of signing of the agreement so there won't be any breach later. The agreement should include that you, as the victim, are not responsible and that all the fraud will be deleted in your name and that the payment in full is complete restitution.

Legal Help

If your family wishes to resolve the issues and help the fraudster to be rehabilitated, consider victim/offender mediation to resolve the emotional as well as financial issues. A mediator can help develop a legally binding agreement with all the family members, help foster healing and forgiveness, and set forth parameters for accountability. Don't expect the creditor to become involved in the mediation, since their only concern is getting paid and this would be a waste of their time.

If your family member or relative committed a crime in your name other than identity theft, you must protect yourself. Never take responsibility for a crime you didn't commit. Follow the steps in Chapter 15.

Spousal Identity Theft

When the identity thief is your spouse or former spouse (during divorce), the situation gets particularly tricky. In most states, the law treats both parties' debts as marital property for which you are jointly held responsible. Your husband or wife had a fiduciary duty to ask your permission before applying for even a joint account using your Social Security number. While you are married, absent a premarital agreement for each of you to keep your property separate, you will be responsible for joint debts. If there is an existing joint bank or credit account, then the spouse would have had the right to do anything with it that you could have done. In other words, under the law, there may have been no fraud at all while you were married and living together. If you are separated, then the situation may be different.

If you are in the middle of a divorce proceeding and no longer in the same residence, identity theft is easier to prove. Identity theft can also be a weapon for one spouse to get revenge against the other. As both a privacy attorney and a family-law attorney, I have seen many cases of mean-spirited identity theft by one spouse attempting to discredit the other and gain advantage in divorce or custody proceedings.

If your spouse is using your Social Security number or stealing your identity, it's time for marital counseling. If that fails, it's time to cut your losses and dissolve the marriage. If you decide to separate, once you live apart, contact the CRAs as Chapter 4 explains. But instead of disputing any of the accounts, explain that you are legally and financially separated from your spouse. Cancel joint accounts, but get your own credit cards first.

You may put a 100-word statement on your account that you are separated and that no joint account is to be issued and that you don't authorize your former spouse to be an authorized user of your accounts. Put a new password on your own accounts. Also, place a fraud alert on your account not to issue credit without calling you first on your cell phone. You may also consider a credit freeze if you are not in need of new credit in the near future

The Least You Need to Know

- It is best to make a police report no matter what, even when you know the identity thief. If you are reluctant to involve law enforcement, confront the person and ask him or her to admit the truth in an affidavit.

- Realistically, if the impostor signs an affidavit and promises to pay, police won't investigate or send a case to the district attorney.

- Before "covering" for a relative, consider that you will have financial losses, your credit will be likely ruined, and you will enable that person to do it again, and you will be angry at yourself as well.

◆ If your spouse uses your Social Security number to apply for credit or services, the fact that you are (or were) married will probably make it challenging to clear up identity theft.

◆ If the spouse's behavior continues and you need to divorce, handle the misuse of your Social Security number as fraud and address it with your family-law attorney.

Part 4

Square Away the Bureaucracies

Beyond the pain of dealing with financial fraud, identity theft can leave you vulnerable to having your official identity corrupted with governmental agencies. You'll learn how to work through some of the biggest bureaucracies and straighten out attacks on your identity with such entities as the Social Security Administration, the IRS, the Veterans Administration, state registries of motor vehicles, and the State Department. If your identity was stolen at work, or if someone is committing fraud under your business name, I have a systematic approach to assist you. And if someone stole your medical identity, there is detailed help to navigate the complexities of insurance companies and deal with healthcare providers.

Chapter

12

Dealing with the Government

In This Chapter

- ◆ Re-establishing your government identification
- ◆ Repairing IRS and state tax shams
- ◆ Recovering government benefits
- ◆ Avoiding fraudulent support demands

Up until this chapter, I've focused primarily on dealing with CRAs, creditors, financial institutions, and other aspects of financial identity theft. But any time you have been the target of identity theft, you need to consider how else you might have been affected. In this chapter, you'll learn how to address the problems in the following three areas:

- ◆ Government IDs
- ◆ Tax agencies
- ◆ Government offered/managed benefits

You'll at least need to consider these issues if you've faced any identity theft. Go through the chapter from top to bottom because the section on the IRS will be affected by what you find out from the Social Security Administration.

Dealing with Government IDs

Victims often find that the fraud has invaded their lives insidiously. You may find the impostor has received governmental benefits, obtained official identification in your name, or, worse yet, has gotten you in trouble with the IRS or state tax authorities.

Information = Power

You may not have found fraud on your credit report but learned of other uses of your identity, such as fraudulently getting a job or using your Social Security number to get governmental benefits. There may have been no overt financial theft, but your identity has still been compromised. Carefully consider to what else you may have been exposed.

Government identification is part of life, whether a document such as a driver's license or passport, or the biggest key to unlocking your identity: your Social Security number. Some impersonators may focus on your personal finances, some use your identity to avoid prosecution for crimes, some want free healthcare, and others just want revenge. Successful impersonators are clever and creative as to the use of your good name and reputation. Here are the major categories you must consider with regard to governmental benefits:

- Social Security card
- Driver's license
- Passport
- Military/veteran IDs
- Security clearance identification
- Professional licenses

You'll take a similar remedial approach to the one in Chapter 4 for dealing with CRAs and creditors. First call the appropriate government entity, follow up by letter (return receipt requested), and provide the following:

- A cover letter addressing how you learned that someone stole your identity

- Your name, Social Security number, and date of birth

- Victim chronology

- Completed FTC affidavit

- Copy of the law-enforcement report and the name and contact information of the law-enforcement agency

- Copy of your driver's license or other government-issued ID, or the identification document involved in the theft (i.e., passport or military ID)

- Copy of a utility bill or bank statement showing your name and address

- Copy of evidence that the government-provided identity card, license, identification, or clearance has been compromised

There is no central government clearinghouse to fix all of your affected government IDs. In addition to the steps I give you, look at each agency's website to obtain new fraud information and possible forms to send along with your letter.

Social Security

If someone has used your Social Security number to get a job or to receive SSI or government disability benefits, you need to alert the Social Security Administration. Telephone the Social Security Office of the Inspector General at its fraud hotline, 1-800-269-0271. Explain that you've been the victim of identity theft and place a fraud alert on your Social Security number. This will keep the SSA from issuing a replacement card at an address other than yours. Then follow up by mail, return receipt requested, to the following address:

Social Security Administration
Fraud Hotline
P.O. Box 17768
Baltimore, MD 21235

Check with the Social Security Administration to obtain your Personal Earnings and Benefit Estimate Statement (PEBES). This document shows the Social Security benefits you've accrued and your documented and reported work history. That history will indicate if someone has been using your Social Security number for employment, because your earnings for each year will be listed on the report. If the earnings are higher than what you know them to be, or otherwise inaccurate, get your copy of your tax return and call 1-800-772-1213 to discuss. The actual employers are not listed on the report, but you can get your free work history at www.ChoicePoint.com as part of your annual free disclosure.

Information = Power

Financial fraud is not in the purview of the Social Security Administration, unless someone is fraudulently obtaining benefits or checks from the SSA. If someone uses your Social Security number to establish new credit, the Social Security Administration has no power to stop the fraud.

You can order your PEBES in a number of ways. The four-page document you receive is titled "Your Social Security Earnings Statement," and the SSA sends a copy to you every year about three months before your birthday.

To order your statement call the SSA at 1-800-772-1213, or visit your local SSA office. You'll need to fill out an SSA-7004 form, also available online at www.socialsecurity.gov. Mail the completed form to:

Social Security Administration
Wilkes Barre Data Operations Center
P.O. Box 7004
Wilkes Barre, PA, 18767-7004

To fill out the form, you'll need the following information:

◆ Name and Social Security number as they appear on your Social Security card

◆ Date of birth

◆ Place of birth

◆ Mother's maiden name (last name only)

It takes four to six weeks if you send the SSA-7004 form in by mail, but only two to four weeks if you submit the request on the website.

If there are any job entries you don't recognize, your impostor may be working in your name, and his or her income may be reported to the tax authorities, so you'll also need to contact the IRS right away, which I discuss later in this chapter.

> ### Information = Power
>
> Although it is possible to be issued a new Social Security number, it is almost never a good idea unless you're doing so for your child who is 16 years of age or younger. (If you have already established financial accounts, such as college tuition funds, or credit under your child's name and Social Security number, you may wish to correct the fraud instead of changing the Social Security number.) In our database-driven society, your old Social Security will link to the new Social Security Number in the CRA files, so you'll look as if you are trying to hide bad credit or a criminal history.

For any fraud or errors, you'll need to correct the record by filing a form SSA-7008, available from an SSA office or from its website. Attach your police report and FTC affidavit to the form and mail it, return receipt requested, to:

Social Security Administration
300 N. Greene Street
Baltimore, MD, 21201

Driver's License

Identity thieves can often get an authentic-looking fake driver's license with your name, but their photo and address, for only $25. Some slick fraudsters are able to go to the DMV and get a "duplicate" authentic license in your name with their own photos.

If the fraudster has received a driver's license in your name with his or her photo, contact your state Department of Motor Vehicles, cancel your license, ask that a new license number be issued to you immediately, and place a fraud alert on your profile with the DMV. Also ask that your driving record and all documents pertaining to the theft be sent to you so you can dispute the record and have it segregated from yours.

In addition to asking for a fraud alert, ask the department to send you a copy of your driving records so you can look for potential traffic or parking offenses on your record that your impostor may have created.

Passport

A passport extends identity theft beyond the borders of this country and could cause you problems when traveling. If someone applies for and obtains a passport in your name, your impersonator could commit a crime in another country, incorrectly making you a wanted person. I was contacted by a CEO of a company who was arrested upon his arrival in Germany for crimes his impostor committed there.

Terrorists (including the 9/11 brigade) have also used falsified passports to accomplish their evil deeds. Imagine being associated with someone like that.

Information = Power

If you are a victim of identity theft and don't have a passport in your name, get one immediately to prevent someone else from beating you to it and getting one in your name first.

There are two ways an identity thief will commit passport fraud: either get a valid driver's license in your name with his or her own photo and then use a forged birth certificate to apply for a passport, or doctor an existing passport by replacing your picture with his or hers.

If you are suspicious that passport fraud has occurred, alert the State Department by phone and follow up by sending a letter with the information at the beginning of the chapter to the following address:

U.S. Department of State
Passport Services
Consular, Lost/Stolen Passport Section
1111 19th Street, NW
Suite 500
Washington, D.C., 20036

Include copies of the identification pages from your travel visa or passport, if you have one. If you don't have a passport, get one, and ask for a fraud alert to be placed on your file. Then ask the Department of State for whatever other steps you should take pursuant to your situation.

Military IDs

When it comes to identity theft, military personnel are easy prey since they often move and may even be deployed out of the country. Furthermore, the military ID number is the person's Social Security number and is printed on their military ID, dog-tags, and other documents. The Department of Defense has said that it will switch all cards to another numbering system in the near future, but it's a big and expensive task, and the personal information has been readily available for service people for a long time.

If you suspect your military ID was used, whether in the U.S. or overseas, immediately report the theft to the nearest military police office as well as to your local community police, if you or your family lives off-base. Then you follow the same steps recommended in this book, depending on the type of fraud.

Even if the military changes your ID to a random number, you are still more vulnerable than others if you are deployed outside the country. So it's a good idea to place a military alert on your credit profile with the CRAs. An active-duty alert is monitored in your file for 12 months. Use the contact information in Chapter 4 to reach the major CRAs.

You will also be removed from pre-screening offers of credit and insurance for two years. I'd also recommend a security freeze to "lock" your credit profile, as Chapter 4 explains.

Identity Crisis

If the military has still not replaced Social Security numbers as the ID number by the time you're reading this, then follow the instructions in Chapter 4 (as well as the part of this chapter dealing with Social Security numbers) to clear your name.

Security Clearance

If a thief has stolen your identity and you have a government security clearance, you need to ensure that the person using your name does not have access to classified material. An impostor used the identity of one of my clients to get government security clearance—which my client found out when the FBI came to his home to arrest him.

Call the agency that issued your clearance and the agency with which the fraudster is involved to explain the situation. Then follow up in writing, including evidence of the fraud. Unfortunately, I have seen clients lose their clearance, presumably because of their failure to prevent the occurrence or address it quickly.

Victims also face another potential clearance problem. If the fraudster had committed crimes and given your identity to law-enforcement officials, you may suddenly find that you have a criminal record, which would prevent you from keeping your clearance.

If you are refused a security clearance, you have a right to see the grounds on which you were denied clearance. A background check and other documents will list the sources of information that led to the denial. Those sources will be information brokers and private investigators who gather information about you. You will need to ascertain each source, including obtaining arrest and court records, if any. Call and write each source and request the documents under your rights as an identity-theft victim according to the Fair Credit Reporting Act (FCRA 609e). Make sure to send your identity-theft report and FTC affidavit with a cover letter (return receipt requested). For more on criminal identity theft, see Chapter 15.

Professional License Fraud

If you're a licensed professional and the fraudster is trying to pass himself or herself off as you in a business context, even if he or she is only passing out business cards with your name on them, you need to contact the state's licensing agency.

Call first and then follow up with a letter, including the necessary explanation and verification documents from the top of this chapter.

You may need to get a new license number unless the licensing board uses your Social Security number. Ask to have a fraud alert placed on your file and request a form to set a password that you can use to change information if necessary. Ask the agency for an accounting of any address changes or complaints against you.

IRS and State Tax Revenue Agencies

We're going to give the IRS its own treatment here. That's because it is a complex bureaucracy that has enormous impact on your life. You may have been affected when someone worked, or won money in Las Vegas, under your Social Security number and didn't or doesn't pay taxes. The IRS and even your state tax board will come after you. A fraudster might have filed a false tax return and received an undeserved refund before you had a chance to file. At the University of California, Irvine, where I teach, more than a hundred graduate students couldn't file their tax returns because impostors had used this last scheme.

Here are some red flags to let you know you may have a tax-fraud problem:

◆ The IRS sends you a letter that you've underreported earnings by a significant amount, although you always report all your income.

◆ Child-support payments were deducted from your tax return, although you don't have kids or owe support.

◆ The IRS tells you that you can't file another tax return because you've already filed one this year.

Should the IRS think that you owe taxes and attempt to collect them, here's what it can do:

◆ Put a lien on your credit report

◆ Freeze bank accounts

◆ Seize property

◆ Garnish wages from your employer

◆ Seize money that customers owe your small business

So if you get a letter from the IRS (or your state tax authority), you must act immediately. Because of its broad powers to collect money owed, your highest priority is to call and deal with the taxing authorities immediately, before any other creditor. Your financial life depends on it!

If someone has used your Social Security number for tax purposes, then you need to call the IRS special identity-theft number, 800-908-4490, and send a follow up letter to the IRS with your police report and affidavit. Also complete IRS form 14039 (available at irs.gov). Include a copy of the letter you sent to the Social Security Administration. Ask for a copy of the tax returns and all documentation and correspondence that they may have regarding the fraud. You may need to visit a local IRS office as part of straightening out the problem.

Identity Crisis

If the PEBES statement from the Social Security Administration shows income that is beyond what you've earned, your letter to the IRS will also need to request any tax status reporting forms, such as W-2s or 1099s, and other tax returns that may have been filed in your name.

Examine the documents received from the IRS, paying attention to the time periods of employment, salaries reported, and any other information that will show you never worked in those positions. You'll need to get contact information for the thief's employers. Call the employers, following up in writing, and request all potential evidence, including job applications and personnel forms.

You'll then need to explain the fraud and notify the IRS and tax authorities in the state in which your impostor worked. Give evidence of your own employment or income during the pay period in question. Provide your paystubs, W-2s, or 1099s during the same time to show that you worked elsewhere. The toll-free IRS assistance number for individuals is 1-800-829-1040. If your fraudster caused problems with your small business, call 1-800-829-4933.

You must contact your state's Department of Revenue and follow similar procedures. The particulars and address will vary with the state, so contact the appropriate agency and request information on how it handles identity theft. You may save time by sending a cover letter with a copy of your letter and attachments which you previously sent to the IRS.

For further help, contact the IRS Taxpayers Advocate Service, an office focused on acting as the representative of taxpayers in the agency. You can find more information at www.irs.gov/advocate. The Contact Your Advocate link will give you the proper contact information for your state's office, or you can call 1-877-777-4778.

Information = Power

Depending on your situation, the IRS Code may help you as a fraud victim. Under US IRS Code 165e, your fraud losses and out-of-pocket expenses due to identity theft may be tax deductible. Show logs of time and expenses, attorney fees, and so on to your accountant to determine what you may deduct during the year(s) you are recovering from the theft.

If you still are having problems, contact the U.S. Treasury Inspector General for Tax Administration (TIGTA), which provides independent oversight of IRS activity. TIGTA can open an investigation if an issue falls into one of three categories, one of which is "external attempts to corrupt tax administration." That includes people fraudulently reporting information. Click the Contact link on the website to find the regional offices as well as contact information for the Fraud and Criminal Intelligence Division.

Tax Liens

The worst-case scenario is if the IRS has filed a lien for money it thinks you owe for taxes. In that case, not only do you need to do all of the above, but also deal with the lien. If the taxing agencies will not take action to remove the lien (which they should do), you will need to contact a tax attorney to help you in the courts.

Your credit reports will show a tax lien and in what court it was filed. Call the court and ask how to get a copy of the entire court file. You'll have to pay for copies unless you can get them electronically.

Part of the record will be the contact information for the lawyer handling the case for the IRS. Contact the lawyers with the details listed at the beginning of this chapter and explain the situation, providing a copy of what you sent to the IRS. You'll need to discuss the steps to remove the lien with both the assigned IRS agent and lawyer. If it is from fraud, the IRS lawyer should do the court paperwork. If the IRS refuses to remove the lien, you will need your own lawyer. See Chapter 16 for details on handling civil court cases and liens, specifically an IRS lien.

Government-Benefits Fraud

One of the more cold-water-in-your-face ways you may learn of identity theft is being told that you are already receiving a benefit to which you've just become entitled, or hearing that you have obligations to support a spouse or child you don't have. Here is how to handle some situations that are, sadly, a new trend for identity-theft victims.

Social Security, Medicare, Medicaid, and Disability

What if you are eligible to apply for Social Security benefits only to have been told that you are already receiving them? You contact the Social Security Administration fraud hotline, mentioned earlier in this chapter, and request the details of what benefits were being paid to your impersonator and to where payments were sent. Then you will dispute the information with your letter, affidavit, police reports, and evidence showing that you've never received benefits. You'll show every discrepancy between you and your evil twin.

For Medicare, you're also dealing with the Social Security Administration and will follow the above steps. States administer Medicaid, so in addition to appealing directly to the Medicaid fraud office in your state, and possibly the state where the swindler lives, you will also need to realize this is medical identity theft and take all measures explained in Chapter 14.

Worker's Comp or Disability Fraud

If you're reading this section, then chances are you got hurt at work and went to the insurance carrier handling your employer's workers' compensation only to hear that you've been denied your right to benefits because you're already receiving them. Or you applied for disability and were denied since your impostor is receiving payments. You'll have to use the techniques in Chapter 8 for dealing with insurance fraud as well as in Chapter 14 for medical identity theft.

Always call the agency involved first and ask for the proper contact concerning fraud. Get the telephone number and address so you can send your evidence of fraud along with your FTC affidavit and police report. Request documentation of the details of care as well as cash payments using the information in Chapter 8. Then use the methods in Chapter 14 to obtain details of the care provided to the fraudster. Dispute the details with the healthcare providers, then go back to the workers' comp carrier and present the discrepancies, including showing that you do not live at the address to which it is sending the checks.

Information = Power

Ask the insurance carrier in writing for documents of the insurance coverage where the fraudster was working. Include your identity-theft report and affidavit. You need to contact your impostor's employer to inform the company of the fraud and get the employer to verify that you are not the person receiving the benefits. The employer will probably get law enforcement to investigate, since the employer, the carrier, and you were defrauded. If the impostor worked under your name, you'll know to contact the SSN Administration and IRS as well.

Veterans' Benefits

If you've been denied any of your veteran benefits, such as education, health, disability, home loan, or pension, because someone else is receiving them, then you'll need to contact the Veteran's Administration. Also contact law enforcement to get your identity-theft report.

You'll need to contact your state agency and also the office of Veterans Benefits Administration (www.vba.va.gov/VBA/). Call 1-800-827-1000 and then follow up with your letter of explanation of denials of benefits, copy of your veteran's card with your photo, your FTC affidavit, and your police report. Ask for an investigation and reinstatement. You may need to hire a lawyer to deal with the VA's general counsel's office to reinstate benefits.

You should also contact the Office of Inspector General (www.va.gov/oig), which accepts complaints of criminal activity, including theft from VA beneficiaries. The OIG doesn't handle cases that it thinks should be handled by other offices, including the VBA, but this way you're covering your bases.

If you're not getting the action you need from the VBA, there is also the Board of Veterans Appeals (www.va.gov/vbs/bva) that gives you a higher authority to challenge any decision based on the actions of your doppelganger.

Should the problem be with healthcare benefits, you'll likely need to get healthcare records so you can prove your point, as Chapter 14 shows. Hopefully, though, you'll be able to do much of your research working with a single healthcare provider organization: the Veteran's Administration.

Child/Spousal Support

I've had clients who have had their checking accounts attached or wages garnished to pay child support for kids they didn't have. Some victims learn that spouses they never had were trying to obtain support payments from them. It's tragic because an innocent spouse has sometimes married an identity thief and lived a sham marriage to an impostor, totally unaware of reality. Even the spouse is defrauded.

If you're accused of failure to pay support, you'll need to contact the entity that has informed you of the problem. It could be your bank, employer, the district attorney's office, or child support office. Any such action will start with a court order for support. Get a copy of the court order. Once you get a copy of the court documents, look for the name and contact number of the attorney or district attorney who represented the impostor's spouse or children on the court filing papers. If the person asking for support represented himself or herself, you will need to contact him or her; that information will be in the court papers.

There is a chance that he or she is an impostor, too. If that is a concern, go directly to the clerk of the court or the judge who issued the order. Write a letter to the judge including your police report, affidavit, and evidence of the fraud. If you have a difficult judge, you may need your own lawyer to ask for help from the lawyer who filed the case. (Also see Chapter 16 on how to deal with the court.)

The Least You Need to Know

- If you learn someone worked under your name, immediately get your earnings and benefit statement from the Social Security Administration and follow up with the IRS.

- For all government-benefit fraud, go to the issuing entity to get evidence and dispute it in writing to clear your name.

- For any suspicion of tax fraud, immediately call the IRS identity-fraud division or the taxpayer-advocate office.

- Government-benefit fraud won't appear on credit reports, so you'll find out through some negative notice.

- Government-benefit fraud won't appear on credit reports, but public records may show suspicious activity, so obtain free annual disclosure from ChoicePoint.

13

Workplace Identity Theft

In This Chapter

- ◆ Recovering your identity stolen at work

- ◆ Taking back your business's identity

- ◆ Eliminating perceived ties to a fraudulent company

Most people consider their workplace trustworthy. They may share information about themselves with co-workers. They willingly provide employers with their Social Security number, and other sensitive information for tax purposes and other legal requirements. And that's exactly what makes identity theft in the workplace so easy.

But the danger doesn't end with employees. Even entire companies, small and large, can find themselves cloned, with identity thieves taking on the business identity for illegal profit or revenge. Sometimes identity thieves will create a fake website for the business, or even a completely fraudulent business, using the victim's credentials, and then go to town. I counseled an ophthalmologist whose bookkeeper opened an eyeglass business under the doctor's professional credentials, ordering and selling prescription glasses—even using his employer's credit!

With all of the sensitive personnel and customer data available, the workplace offers identity thieves all the tools they need.

If you're an employee victim of identity theft, pay extra attention to the first section of this chapter. If the fraudster took the identity of your own business, or even created a business in your name, read the second section of the chapter.

Theft of Employee Identities

There are many ways that employees find their identity stolen at work. I've seen all of the following happen:

♦ A former boss takes your Social Security number and applies for credit cards. (This is what happened to Linda Foley, who founded the Identity Theft Resource Center.)

♦ A part-time employee with access to storage rooms takes old payroll records home and commits high-volume identity theft against hundreds of former employees.

♦ A new cleaning crew for an office building is actually an international fraud gang that spends evenings rifling through desks, trash, and unsecured cabinets to pilfer sensitive data.

♦ Unscrupulous employees pull vast amounts of sensitive employee information after breaking into unlocked cabinets or into the computer networks of a corporation.

No matter how it happens, you'll need to recover your identity using the step-by-step approach outlined in Chapters 3 and 4, and then any other chapters that apply to your situation. However, there are some interesting twists you should consider.

In many states, employers have considerable liability if an employee's information is stolen due to careless procedures of the employer. A company could be liable for theft of an employee's ID in a number of ways, including negligent hiring, negligent supervision of employees, negligent access, or careless security procedures.

If you become a victim of fraud because your employer failed to protect you, carefully consider your approach to the situation. You could sue the company, but, realistically, you'd likely lose your job and be black-balled by other companies.

On the other hand, a reputable employer will help you restore your identity. At the very least, your employer may handle the expenses of recovering your identity, and give you paid time off to write letters and make phone calls.

Hidden Agenda

When I was on *48 Hours*, a producer told me that when CBS hired a cleaning crew that turned out to be a Nigerian fraud ring that took information to steal the identity of 20 of the correspondents, the network wrote letters on behalf of the victims, and helped them regain their good names.

ID Theft of Businesses

Thieves can steal the identity of a business as easily as that of a person—and often more easily. You may experience business ID theft in the following ways:

- ◆ You're a small business owner.

- ◆ You run a large business as an executive.

- ◆ You don't own a business but you've been getting collection letters claiming that a company in your name owes money, or you learn that it has ruined your reputation.

You'll need a rehabilitative approach to resolve the fraud problems if you own or run an affected business. If you have no business (or you own a different business), you'll need to totally eradicate any appearance of that fraudulent business.

Businesses

If you own a small business, then you face some sticky issues. If your personal credit cards are involved in financing the business, the fraudster may have charged goods to those cards, involving your personal finances. It's easy to miss those items on your credit-card statement if you have employees using the card for various business purposes.

Far worse is if a fraudster has applied for a new credit card using your personal credit to obtain business lines of credit in order to steal your funds. If the fraudster applies for personal credit cards in your name, you will find them on your credit reports in both the inquiries and account section. Use Chapters 2, 3, and 4 to rehabilitate your identity.

The worst case, however, is if the fraudster has applied for business credit cards and credit lines. You won't find the accounts displayed on your credit reports. The FCRA does not apply to business accounts, so credit cards in the name of a business will not appear on your credit bureau reports as accounts.

Things get more complicated when the credit cards and accounts are business credit-card accounts because those accounts are not reported to the CRAs. (However, remember that the creditors will probably get access to your credit profile and many do account reviews, so check out the inquiry section of your credit reports for inquiries from companies unknown to you.) In fact, it's only recently in the state of California, where I live, that the legislature made it possible for a business to file police reports for identity theft.

Identity Crisis

Fraudsters are getting savvy to this and are applying for business accounts to make it less likely that you will discover the accounts until collection companies buy them after the impostor has racked up thousands of dollars in your name.

If your business was victimized, you'll need to look at the reports of Dunn & Bradstreet, a major source of business credit information, which sells reports on companies, including reports of late payments from creditors. D&B also has a service that allows small businesses to monitor their credit reports for a fee, so you can see if there are indications that someone is doing business under your company's name.

Because there are no laws requiring action on the part of D&B for victims of business fraud, you will need to use a combination of evidence, persuasion, and the techniques and approaches in this book to get cooperation. It is vital to get the details that will allow you to learn which companies are reporting fraudulent accounts and late payments. Then can you go to those companies to dispute the account and resolve the problem. The larger your company, the more leverage you'll be able to exert to clear the situation. Of course, you'll eventually find out about the fraudulent accounts when collection agencies contact you for payment.

> **Information = Power**
>
> A great deal of business identity theft happens on the Internet. If someone has constructed a website claiming to be yours, sending out fake e-mails in your business name or otherwise creating cyber-grief for you, see Chapter 17.

Consumers and Fraudulent Companies

If you're a consumer and a fraudster has identified you as the owner of a fake business, you probably didn't learn about the identity theft until you started getting collection letters from companies. Chances are you assumed that previous payment inquiries were just pre-screened offers of credit.

There is good news and bad news. The bad news is that you're unlikely to find any of the fraudulent accounts on your credit reports. However, you will find inquiries in those reports that show which companies have accessed your credit profile.

The good news is that because you are not a business owner but rather a consumer, you are entitled to the protections of the FCRA and have the right to receive evidence of the fraud and to delete the fraud information from your credit reports.

Now use the techniques in Chapters 3 and 4, as well as appropriate others, and insist that the companies treat the case as one involving a consumer. Get copies of your credit reports and look for the hard-pull or hard-report section. Carefully scrutinize the listings. If you don't recognize a company as one from which you wished to get credit, call the company and ask their credit department why it accessed your credit report. Ask for the copy of the application and get a name and address of the fraud department. Follow up with a letter requesting copies of all documentation of the fraud and also ask that the account be denied or closed.

You won't be able to dispute accounts that have not been reported to the CRAs; you can dispute only the inquiries. Dispute the accounts directly with the companies who issued the credit.

The Least You Need to Know

- ◆ If fraudsters get your identity through your employer, it's wiser to ask it for help to recover rather than suing.

- ◆ Business owners should treat any fraud as though it were against them personally and separate from business account fraud so they can retain legal rights under the FCRA.

- ◆ If you believe there are fraudulent business accounts, check out your business credit history at Dunn & Bradstreet's website (dnb. com).

- ◆ If someone has started a fraudulent business in your name, get all documents of the fraud from creditors and search the Internet for information about the fraudulent business name to see what information is available.

Chapter 14

Prescription for Recovery

In This Chapter

- ◆ What medical identity fraud is
- ◆ How it affects you
- ◆ How recovering from medical identity fraud is different
- ◆ How to clear your name and your medical records

Few people enjoy heading to the doctor's office, let alone the hospital, and no one likes writing checks for medical insurance, co-pays, or exorbitant bills. But if you're reading this chapter, then you may have been contacted by a healthcare provider—whether doctor, hospital, clinic, medical testing lab, pharmacy, home nursing firm, or medical device company—or collection agency asking you to pay a bill for care you never needed or received. Your insurance company might have sent a form explaining some treatment you never actually had, or you have seen collection accounts for healthcare bills on your credit reports.

You may be dealing with something more invasive and painful than a root canal: medical identity theft.

Medical Identity Theft: The Big Picture

Medical identity theft is easy to pull off. After all, when's the last time you had to give anything other than some easy-to-find personal information to a healthcare provider, even one that you haven't seen before? If you have health insurance that handles payments, you might not even know about the problem until it reaches a more advanced state, like a bill going into collections.

> **Legal Lingo**
>
> **Medical identity theft** happens when someone uses your identity to get healthcare in your name and contaminates medical records in your name with conditions, procedures, medicines, treatments, prescriptions, and other healthcare that you have not had. The impostor escapes paying the bills and saddles you with medical debt and false diagnoses, which could cause financial and possible health challenges for you. (For groundbreaking medical identity research see www.wordprivacyforum.org/medicalidentitytheft.)

Now, not every mistake in billing or wrongly attributed procedure is deliberate identity theft. Plain old mistakes happen. In this chapter, I'm going to explain how you can find out what occurred, how it could affect you, and how to cure the problem.

If you think this is more complicated than our process of handling financial fraud, you're right. That's because medical identity theft can hurt you in multiple ways:

 ◆ Healthcare providers or collection agencies might try getting you to pay someone else's bills.

♦ Some health insurance plans might treat the charges as part of an annual or overall coverage ceiling, reducing your benefits—or even assume that you hadn't reported a pre-existing condition and cancel your policy.

♦ If you get sick, healthcare providers might incorrectly diagnose your condition because of the fraudster's medical problems being included in your history.

♦ You may be denied such things as the chance to drive a car or get a pilot's license, operate heavy machinery, or be hired for certain types of jobs, or you may not be able to get life or disability insurance depending on the misdiagnosis.

♦ The wrong piece of information in your medical history, like treatment of a drug overdose, could cause unwelcome attention by law-enforcement agencies.

You have to be sure that none of this fraud lingers to cause you a problem, even if all you've experienced thus far are credit issues. But don't panic. Even if your problem spreads to your medical identity, you'll be able to solve it. You'll find that you've learned important facts about your health and the system that will also empower you to protect yourself in the future.

Recovering your medical identity can be more complicated than a case of financial identity theft, where there are established steps to remedy the problem. In some ways, medical identity theft is similar to new account fraud, in that the impersonator uses your purloined identity and creates a shadow "you" to obtain goods and services. The financial fraudster gets credit; the medical fraudster gets credit *and* medical care.

However, even though medical identity theft is similar to creating new credit accounts, it's also significantly different. CRAs only show signs of fraud if healthcare providers assign unpaid charges to collection agencies, so you rarely see the early warning signs of inquiries on your credit record that might otherwise display with financial identity theft. Healthcare accounts won't appear until they are sold to collections (see Chapter 4).

There is no medical equivalent to CRAs with central reporting agencies, so there is no practical way to set a fraud alert on your name to prevent medical services for a fraudster who may create false medical records in your name. There is also no way to freeze your medical records and no way to force providers to contact you before administering care.

In addition, federal privacy law can actually make it difficult to see what happened and track down the perpetrator. (More on this later in this chapter.) So you need a clean-up approach specifically tailored for medical identity theft to handle the crossed boundaries between credit bureaus, the healthcare industry, and government. Here are the general steps you'll use:

1. Order your credit reports.

2. Check insurance industry records.

3. Get records from specific insurers.

4. Get your own medical records from your providers that show your true health history.

5. Profile the problem by obtaining records created by fraudster.

6. Make a law-enforcement report.

7. Correct the records.

8. Monitor your condition.

Information = Power

Although fixing medical identity theft is complicated, you can save time by overlapping steps. Make a police report including financial and medical identity theft, always put a fraud alert on your credit reports, and obtain copies of your credit profile and healthcare records, and fraudulent records at the same time.

Get the Evidence

In the worst-case scenario, you're going to need to correct multiple areas of your identity: financial, insurance, and medical. So I'll walk you through how to get the documents you need, what information to look for, and how to build a case to support your claim of identity theft.

The Health Insurance Portability and Accountability Act (HIPAA) is a federal law that governs how the healthcare world manages paper and electronic records. Under HIPAA, insurers and healthcare providers can only charge you expenses to copy the files, though medical records can easily run dozens of pages and x-rays can be expensive to duplicate unless they are transferred electronically. At the very least, get X-ray, CT scan, and other written reports. If you need the actual images of scans, X-rays, and ultrasounds, you can have the actual hard copies or digital files sent to your doctor.

Hidden Agenda

HIPAA is a very complex law that also deals with privacy and security issues. One provision allows you to obtain a copy of your healthcare records from almost any provider. The right does not, however, extend to psychotherapy notes, other mental health records, some records regarding you or your impostor's participation in medical research, prison medical records, and some laboratory records. Records created in anticipation of litigation may also be considered privileged.

Order Your Credit Reports

Your credit reports won't always be affected by medical identity theft if the fraudster has paid the bills. Many impostors will use your insurance and pay the co-pay, hoping you won't notice on your statements from your carrier. That's why it's so important to review your insurance statements. For example, if no one has reported unpaid accounts to any of the CRAs, then you won't see anything on the credit report. But you need to check anyway, using the detailed approach in Chapter 4.

If there are delinquent medical collection accounts on your credit report, use the information in Chapter 4 to remove it. Those accounts will lead you to important information for the rest of your medical identity theft investigation.

You'll need the name, address, and phone number of every healthcare provider, which you may obtain from the debt-collection companies on your credit report. You may not recognize the providers if they treated the fraudster, so check your credit header information on your credit report to see if there is an address or phone number you don't recognize that the fraudster may have supplied to the healthcare provider.

Identity Crisis _____

Call the healthcare provider to find out where bills were originally sent. If the address information for you is wrong, then you'll need to see if the perpetrator provided a fake address and phone number, or leased an apartment or house and opened utility accounts in your name at that address. Look at Chapter 8 for details on how to do this.

If there is fraud on your credit report, it will indicate medical collection accounts, but it will not show any medical information because that would be a violation of FCRA.

Check Insurance Industry Records

Because health insurance companies pay for much of the medical service provided in this country, you'll need to get information from them. First you need to know which insurers to contact. There's yours, but the fraudster may have created an account at another insurer.

Legal Lingo _____

The **Medical Information Bureau (MIB)** is a medical insurance databank used by nearly 500 insurance companies in the United States and Canada. The records apply to those who have applied for health insurace as an individual, not a group plan. It lets the insurers share health information to verify patient data about your medical profile. This helps them exclude a pre-existing condition when changing insurance carriers.

Start by going to the *Medical Information Bureau (MIB)*, which is considered a specialty consumer-reporting agency under the Fair Credit Reporting Act. This means that you can get a copy of the report free once every year at www.mib.com, and you have the right to dispute errors, have the MIB investigate by notifying the carriers who reported the mistakes/fraud, and have the erroneous data deleted from your file.

The MIB is contacted by member life, health, disability, or critical illness insurance companies when they are establishing an account for someone. If you or the fraudster using your identity have applied for life, health, or disability insurance in the last seven years, there may be an MIB consumer record for you.

Your MIB record can have three different types of information: details of medical history and treatment associated with you, a list of insurance companies that reported the details of medical history and treatment, and a list of all insurers that received a copy of your file during the last 12 months. The details of medical history and treatment become part of the information you'll sift later in the chapter for evidence of fraud or error.

The lists of insurance companies either reporting those medical details or receiving a copy of your file will become the carriers from whom you seek additional information, as you'll see detailed in the next section.

Once a year you can request a free copy of your MIB consumer file by calling 1-866-692-6901 or going to www.mib.com. When you call, you will be asked for personal identification information. You'll need to certify under penalty of perjury that the information you provide is accurate.

Identity Crisis

If you see an insurance company you've never heard of either reporting on you or asking for your file, it's a strong sign that someone is creating accounts under your name.

Get Healthcare Provider Records

Once you learn what healthcare providers reported to insurance companies, you'll need to get their records. Each healthcare agency and health insurer's *notice of privacy practices* becomes the guideline that tells you how to ask for and get information from them. Every entity may have different procedures, so you need to get a notice of your rights and their privacy practices from each entity.

The *listing of benefits* shows everything that the specific insurance carrier has paid in your name, as well as the healthcare provider that performed the service. If the identity thief has changed your address and phone number, you would not have seen the bills. The same is true if someone has used your identity to create an account with a different insurer, which may happen if the person gets a job with healthcare benefits in your name or applies for Medicaid or Medicare using your identity. The listing will also let you see which healthcare providers have been specifically paid by the insurance company.

> **Legal Lingo**
>
> A **notice of privacy practices** explains what information is collected, how it is used, with whom it may be shared, how you may get it, how much it may cost, and how you may obtain your records. A **listing of benefits** is a document that shows what services, treatments, medicines, and devices the healthcare insurance carrier paid for on your behalf.

As you go through the listing of insurance benefits, specifically look for treatments, doctors visits, medicines, hospitalizations, medical devices, tests, or anything else that you cannot remember getting. Circle those benefits and the associated healthcare providers that don't pertain to you. Now you're ready to get your medical records.

Get Your Medical Records

Your medical records show the details of illnesses and conditions, diagnoses made, and care or treatment provided, listing the specific people who were involved with the care, including doctors, nurses, radiologists, pharmacists, physical therapists, dentists, and so on. Every healthcare provider generates medical records for its patients.

> **Information = Power**
>
> Healthcare records are often confusing, and two providers' records for the same person will almost never have identical information. You need to obtain your record from every provider and insurer that you have used first. This is important to prove your true medical history and see if there is any fraud in those files. You'll also need to get medical records in your name from other organizations that treated the impersonator so that you will be able to dispute the fraudulent entries.

Just as you did with the insurance companies, start by asking each provider for a notice of privacy practices. Under HIPAA, every provider must give a copy of its notice to anyone who asks. First search the provider's website, as it may have the notice of privacy practices and how you can access your record. If not, call the provider and ask for the steps and forms to obtain records. Under HIPAA, the provider has 30 days to act on your request.

Remember to keep track of your out-of-pocket costs. Also, most healthcare offices now have their most recent records in electronic form, so you can ask them to send the electronic files to you encrypted with a password. Those should be sent at very little cost.

At this early stage, don't let the healthcare provider know you are a victim of ID theft. One problem in getting your healthcare records is that HIPAA can become as much of a problem as a help. Under the law, healthcare providers, insurance companies, and other entities aren't allowed to disclose someone's medical information to an unauthorized party. Guess what? If you tell a healthcare provider upfront that your record includes data about someone other than you (your impostor), the provider or insurer legally cannot disclose that privileged information. When it comes to the fraudster, you're considered an unauthorized party, even though we're talking about a record in your name.

The way to work around this is not to say a single word about fraud at first. Just say, *"I need copies of all medical records and billing statements in my name, please. How do I obtain those?"* You legally needn't say anything more, so don't.

Once you have the records, scrutinize the following information:

- ◆ Patient's name, address
- ◆ Descriptive data, such as age, gender, height, weight
- ◆ Basic medical data, like blood type
- ◆ Description of the patient's condition
- ◆ Diagnoses, prescriptions, and procedures
- ◆ Date and location of service

If the descriptive data (address, age, blood type, and so on) does not match yours, you have evidence of fraud.

Identity Crisis

Medical jargon is difficult to read and you'll need help. You can go to a site like WebMD.com, search terms in your record, and see what comes up, or just Google the diagnosis and call your own physician to confirm.

If you don't understand a diagnosis, ask the provider. And if you see records from your own provider or don't recognize a procedure, don't automatically assume the worst. It's surprisingly easy to completely forget about something you had done years before, and a provider might have made an error that must be corrected.

In all cases, talk to the specific healthcare providers who were involved with the treatment in question. Call the healthcare provider (you may be able to go there if it's local) and ask for the records. Then ask to speak to the treating professional and get as much specific detail about the person claiming to be you as possible, and send a summary letter to confirm what was said. Ask questions including, but not limited to, the following:

♦ What did the person look like? What was his/her height, weight, hair color, or race, if not in the record? Were there any tattoos or piercings? Was the person right- or left-handed?

♦ Did the person complete a form as to where he or she lived or worked?

♦ Did the person provide marital status, friends, associates, customary activities, or frequented locations?

♦ Did the person talk with an accent, have any unusual pronunciation, or use any slang or jargon?

♦ Was the person wearing any distinctive clothing or jewelry?

Take copious notes and, if you learn a great deal about the fraudster, document the conversation in a thank-you note to the healthcare provider and ask him or her for help in correcting the files to show it was not you. The provider will be worried that he or she has legal liability, so unless there was a conspiracy, just let the provider know you want help in getting back your life, and you want to help law enforcement get the criminal.

The truth is, if the providers are helpful to you, they are mitigating their own liability. If they're not and they were negligent in treating someone who used your name, you may have a right to a legal action against them. If you can't get the information you need from the healthcare providers, you may need to write a letter requesting the information. You should attach your police report, FTC affidavit, and evidence of your identity, and reiterate your rights as a victim to get this information under FCRA 609e. If that fails, look at Chapter 18 and consider legal help.

Profile the Problem

As with other types of identity theft, you have to become your own private investigator. Summarize the problem and be sure to concisely compare and contrast your impersonator's characteristics with your own. Assemble everything you've learned from the healthcare providers and the MIB file and put all the data, along with copies of records, into a ring binder. You'll need a divider to split the binder into two categories: "Mistakes" and "Fraud."

Medical record mistakes are difficult to challenge, because the healthcare providers aren't comfortable changing medical records. If the record was correct for the patient who was treated, albeit an impostor, the treatment and diagnosis for that criminal was most likely correct as to the procedures. There is a dilemma for the healthcare providers, especially if the fraudster returns for treatment. For malpractice concerns as well as standard protocol, healthcare providers will add an amendment to the file rather than delete information. The process will be clarified below.

Create a single master list of all the fraudulent information from all of the healthcare records. For each fraudulent use of care, you want to list the discrepancies of the following:

◆ Date and location of care

◆ Such basic medical facts as height, weight, and blood type

- Pre-existing conditions or other pertinent facts

- Nature of diagnosis

- Procedure performed, service rendered, or drug or product used

- Name and contact information for the specific person who provided the service

- All information you gleaned about the fraudster from talking to the people who actually provided the care

Now go down the master list of fraudulent service, concentrating on two things. First, look for information about a given care event or activity that can prove you were not the recipient. For example, if a record lists the recipient as having blood type O+ when you actually have A-, then that's proof you aren't the person being mentioned. Did the impostor use an address that was not yours? Was care given in a place or at a time when you can prove (through receipts or other paperwork) that you could not have been there? Did the patient take a medicine to which you are highly allergic, without any negative effect? Did the fraudster sign a form and leave a signature obviously different from yours? Look for every possible logical inconsistency that can prove your point.

> **Information = Power**
>
> Remember that you may have multiple medical records covering a single provision of care, because it could involve a variety of providers, including doctors, testing labs, and pharmacies. Group all related information together. List treatment as many times as necessary if numerous providers treated the fraudster in various ways.

The second thing you look for are grouped records, where more than one provider is involved with a single incident. Are there inconsistencies, like a doctor authorizing one test and a lab doing another more expensive test? Or do two healthcare providers have data that would describe different people?

Clear Your Name

Don't start this step until you've received all the reports you requested and had time to go through them and compile your evidence. When you've pulled together all your proof that you were not the person receiving care, it's time to go to law enforcement.

Law-Enforcement Report

If you didn't already make an identity-theft report when you first learned of the theft through bills or other evidence, call your local law-enforcement agency immediately to inform them of the crime.

Follow the detailed directions in Chapter 3 to prepare the FTC affidavit (available in Appendix C) and to file an identity-theft report with the appropriate law-enforcement bodies (any local, state, or federal law enforcement). The identity-theft report and your FTC-completed affidavit will make it easier to correct the records.

Correct the Financial Records

When you have the law-enforcement report and the FTC affidavit, you must both call and write each healthcare provider that established the fraudulent records (return receipt requested). If your impostor's treatment created collection efforts against you, follow the steps to clear fraudulent debts with collections agencies using Chapter 6. Ask the collection agency to send you all billing statements and to cease collection efforts. You'll proceed with the financial fraud using the FCRA.

Correct the Diagnostic and Medical Records

To correct your healthcare file. You'll need to do the following:

Send a letter to the providers of the fraudster explaining the fraud and providing the evidence of what you learned above. If the impersonator used any of your own healthcare providers or your own insurance, some of the records will be accurate and the rest will be inaccurate because of the fraudster's activity. Request that the amended hard copy and computer records identify you as the victim of fraud in a narrative statement explaining that the impostor corrupted your medical records.

The fraudulent diagnosis and treatment must be penciled through (deleted with tracked changes in electronic files) and flagged as provided to an impostor. The person correcting the file should indicate the date as well as the name and employee number of the person who made the change. Ask that the provider give you a copy of the written, amended report; acknowledge that the amended record was sent to all those who received the records; and provide you an accounting of the disclosures.

If the impostor received medical care from providers who you never used, none of the record will pertain to you. Therefore, it is imperative that you request in writing (return receipt requested, attaching your identity-theft report and FTC affidavit) that your name, birth date, and Social Security number and insurance policy number be crossed out or deleted with changes tracked in an electronic document. Request that a written explanation clarifying that the entire health record belonged to an impersonator be included in the record and that a copy be sent to you as well as all entities that received the record.

Get an Accounting of Disclosures

Ask for an *accounting of disclosures,* because the healthcare provider may have disclosed your file to individuals or institutions and you need to follow the trail of information to ensure that it is corrected at every step.

HIPAA gives the provider 60 days to make the necessary corrections to your record. But the provider can take an additional 30 days so long as it sends you a written reason for the delay.

If the healthcare provider refuses to amend your record, file a Statement of Disagreement with the provider, concisely explaining the fraud. Include your phone number, the police report number, and the phone number of the officer that took the report. Demand that the provider annotate the file to reflect the fraud and that the statement be attached to your file and sent to all those who have received your file and receive it in the future. In addition, file a fraud complaint with local,

> **Legal Lingo**
>
> An **accounting of dis-closures** is a list of persons or institutions that received your healthcare information from the provider, the date on which the disclosure happened, details of what information was shared, and why the provider shared it.

state, and federal agencies that oversee the healthcare provider. Call the Department of Health and Human Services (866-627-7748) or visit www.hhs.gov/ocr/hipaa.consumer. Refer to 45 C.F.R. §§ 164.508, 164.524, and 164.526. Contact the World Privacy Forum at www.worldprivacyforum.org for up-to-date information on patient privacy rights and medical identity theft.

◆ Contact your health insurance carrier and ask to speak to the fraud department. Alert them to the fraud and ask that they assist you; no insurance carrier wants to pay fraudulent claims.

◆ Contact your state attorney general's office.

◆ Hire a private attorney to help you clear your record.

A healthcare provider or insurer covered under HIPAA is not required to change your record if it thinks that the record is accurate and complete, which is why your police report and detailed evidence of fraud are so important. If the record is not available to you under HIPAA rules (remember that point about privacy of the thief's medical information), or if it did not create the record, they cannot change it. In the first two cases, start going up the organizational ladder and push to amend the record with your request for amendment, the identity-theft report, the affidavit, and a statement clarifying the dispute.

Be persistent. Every time someone at the healthcare provider refuses to amend the record, talk to that person's supervisor. If necessary, you can walk your way all the way up to the CEO's office. You'd be surprised at how quickly problems can get resolved when the head of the organization starts asking why things haven't previously been handled. Also, you can create some incentive for the healthcare provider to make the needed changes through the following:

◆ Call and write your state or federal legislators for help.

◆ Call your local newspapers and tell them your story. It's amazing how media attention can clear your identity theft.

◆ Call a privacy or healthcare attorney for assistance.

Monitor Your Situation

On an ongoing basis, you need to make sure that your healthcare providers will give you proper treatment. If there has been significant fraud, you might find that the illegal use of your insurance reduces the coverage needed for your treatment, whether a procedure or even a prescription. Keep all medical receipts in a file and then, at least once a year, ask your insurer to provide a complete listing of benefits so you can see what payments it has made on your behalf. Compare the list with your receipts. Any payouts to providers on your behalf that you don't recognize are potential signs of additional fraud. Also check your insurance history annually for free at www.mib.com.

The Least You Need to Know

◆ Medical identity theft happens when someone associates your identity with medical care that you never received.

◆ Medical identity theft will only appear on your credit reports if the impostor has not paid the bills and the accounts have gone to collections.

◆ Compare information from your true medical records to that from the fraudster's profile to prove that you didn't receive the treatment services or medicine.

◆ Monitor your ongoing medical records and the MIB to avoid future fraud and correct treatment in the future by your own healthcare providers.

5

Where the Going Gets Tough

Although the law is firmly on your side, you may have challenges proving who you are and exerting your rights. Criminal identity theft can literally threaten your freedom and make you the target of law enforcement and the courts. Or you could find that your impostor caused you to be sued civilly. You'll learn how to deal with lawyers and the courts.

You'll also learn the tricks of dealing with your identity theft when entities affected by the fraud are uncooperative. You'll learn techniques to persuade or escalate issues to get the help you need. Finally, there's information on how to deal with the prosecutor of the perpetrator if he or she is found, and what you can do to safeguard your identity so it is not stolen again.

15

When You Become the Criminal

In This Chapter

◆ Research criminal activities associated with your identity

◆ Enlisting law enforcement in your cause

◆ Clearing your name with law enforcement, district attorneys, courts, and commercial data brokers

Rectifying financial identity theft is time consuming and can be very frustrating. But it's far worse when your thief has committed other crimes in your name leaving you with a criminal record. Suddenly it's not just creditors demanding money. Now you have warrants for your arrest or a conviction record to explain to potential employers. You have to prove your innocence to law enforcement and the courts.

A false criminal record can keep you from getting a job, renewing professional licenses, getting a security clearance if you work in the defense or intelligence industries, and, worst of all, can literally threaten your freedom. Your sham record could even show that you have served time in jail for a crime you never committed.

Obviously, you need to clear your criminal records, and this chapter will help you do that. Just be warned that you'll need to become your own investigator and convince law enforcement to help you.

You're Put on the Spot

When impostors commit *criminal identity theft* using your name, they may have used your identity for financial gain, but their primary objective is to avoid arrest or prosecution.

> **Legal Lingo**
>
> **Criminal identity theft** occurs when a thief steals another's identity, using it, often with a fraudulent driver's license, to commit crimes. When the thief is arrested, or investigated by law enforcement for some violation, they assume that the false identity is the real one. When released on bail, the thief will fail to show up for a hearing and the authorities look for the victim. The unsuspecting victim is saddled with a warrant for arrest. Worse, sometimes the criminal is prosecuted and convicted using the victim's name, thus leaving the victim with a conviction record.

An identity thief can appear to be perpetrator of his or her illegal acts by just using your name and maybe your Social Security number. Law enforcement may take a mug shot, fingerprints, and do a background check. If you have never committed a crime, the background check will show a clean slate and won't have the picture or fingerprints that would show you and the thief to be two different people. If the perpetrator hasn't committed a crime before, or if his fingerprints aren't in the FBI database that is reviewed by law enforcement, when he uses your name, your name will be attributed to his fingerprints in the FBI national database.

You now have a criminal-justice problem. Your first indication of this crime against you may be that you couldn't get a job or were even fired from a job because of your fraudulent criminal record. Maybe you were stopped for speeding and arrested on the spot because of an outstanding warrant actually issued for your evil double. Or you might have ordered your own background check from an information broker (detailed in Chapter 8) and found a criminal conviction or arrest record.

Dealing with Criminal Charges

Unraveling a case of criminal identity theft is similar to tracking down financial identity theft, in the sense that you must be your own investigator:

1. File an impersonation/identity-theft law-enforcement report with your local agency, asking it to send your photo and fingerprints to the arresting agency.

2. Obtain the records from the law-enforcement agency or court that dealt with the fraudster and possesses the files explaining the facts of the arrest or conviction.

3. Use those records to prove your innocence.

4. Contact the appropriate police, prosecutors, and courts to obtain all available information in files with your name.

5. Ask for help from the above entities to analyze contradictions and compile facts that prove your innocence.

6. Engage help from the law-enforcement agency and prosecutors to help you rectify the errors.

7. Correct all the government and commercial databases.

Identity Crisis

If you face problems with criminal identity theft, there is a good chance the thief has also committed financial fraud under your identity. Check for potential financial fraud on your credit reports as Chapter 4 explains.

Collecting Information

You can't correct your criminal profile until you know what charges you are facing or what convictions you allegedly suffered. In criminal identity theft, you need entirely different records than you would for financial identity theft. You will need a *criminal background check*.

> **Legal Lingo**
>
> A **criminal background check** is a document that shows the arrests, warrants, convictions, jail time served, and probation that a person has undergone.

If you learned of your supposed crime from a background check run by a prospective employer who used a third-party information broker, you have a right to get a copy of that report. It will show the source of the record of the arrest warrant or conviction.

If you are unable to get a copy from an employer, you'll need to get your own complete background check. (See Chapter 8 for additional information.) The National Association of Professional Background Screeners website (www.napbs.com) lets you search by location for people who can perform such a check for you. The National Association of Security and Investigative Regulators (www.nasir.org/licensing.htm) and the National Association of Legal Investigators (www.nalionline. org) both list private investigators by geographic area.

> **Information = Power**
>
> Whenever you apply for a job and authorize a background check, ask at the outset to have a copy of the report provided to you when the prospective employer obtains it. Federal law guarantees your right to see the report if prepared by a third party. If prepared in-house by the employer, you don't have that right in most states, but should ask up front for a copy.

If you have convinced your local law-enforcement agency of your innocence, you may also persuade them to provide you a free copy of your criminal background check. When you go to your local law-enforcement agency to get your identity-theft victim report, explain the situation and ask them to do the following:

◆ Run a live scan of your fingerprints in the FBI database.

◆ Run a national criminal search for your name, your Social Security number, and your live-scan fingerprints in their own criminal background check databases.

◆ Take a digital photo of you to send along with your fingerprints to the law-enforcement agency that arrested the real perpetrator to show that the perpetrator is not you.

Information = Power

Because the FBI national database of criminals is not based on the Social Security number but, rather, on fingerprints, if your impostor was fingerprinted, his or her prints won't match yours. If the impostor was arrested in another county or state, you need to have your prints and a photo sent electronically by your local law-enforcement agency to the agency where the real perpetrator committed his or her crime.

Once you obtain your background report, call the information broker who issued the report and follow up in writing to notify it that you are a victim of criminal identity theft. Background-checking companies are also subject to the Fair Credit Reporting Act. In the letter, detail all the errors and ask for a reinvestigation under FCRA 15 U.S.C. 1681. Attach your FTC affidavit and identity-theft report. The background report should show the source of the information, so the information broker should be able to provide you contact information to contact the source, like the court that reported a conviction. Go to the source of the information to get the records.

File a Criminal Identity-Theft Report

Although you may fear arrest and imprisonment, going to the police is vital in getting the justice system to help you. Your local law-enforcement agency is your best ally. Contact your local police to make an impersonation or identity-theft report. If at first they are suspicious of you, don't get angry or upset. Be prepared with plenty of evidence and they will want to get the fraudster. Provide extensive proof of your identity, including government-issued IDs, birth certificate, Social Security card, FTC affidavit, and evidence of your address.

This information, when compared with the photo and prints of the thief, will show that you are not the impostor.

Information = Power

If you're arrested for your double's crime, be cooperative and ask to file your own impersonation report. Just be aware almost everyone who is arrested says, "It wasn't me." Whatever you do, avoid belligerence so they will help you.

Get the Details

To defend yourself, you need all the specifics of what happened. Your local law enforcement can help you get arrest records and documents from the other agencies. Make friends with that investigator any way you honestly can, so he or she will make phone calls to other agencies on your behalf. The more evidence you provide to your investigator, the more assistance you'll get.

Prepare a very appreciative follow-up letter to your investigator, return receipt requested, referring to your impersonation report number. Explain what you know of the fraud, attaching your FTC affidavit. Request that, pursuant to FCRA 609e, you should be provided all evidence of the fraud so that you can repair your good name. Ask the investigator to get a copy of the entire booking record in your name from the agency that handled the fraudster, including mug shot and fingerprints.

If law enforcement already handed the case to the district attorney or federal prosecutors, you'll have to contact the prosecutors and the courts. Here is the list of what you will need to address:

◆ Arrest warrants

◆ Court verdicts

◆ Government databases

◆ Commercial databases

If an impostor was convicted in your name, contact the clerk of the court where the trial or plea bargain took place and ask for the complete file of the case. You'll need to provide the identity-theft report and FTC affidavit; you'll need to pay for copies of the records. Ask for electronic files; as many courts scan records, this should save time and money.

Cleaning Up Your Record

Now we get to step 6, which can get complex. There are five groups you might have to deal with:

♦ Law enforcement

♦ District attorneys or federal prosecutors

♦ Courts

♦ Government agencies

♦ Commercial data brokers

Law Enforcement

Hopefully the local law-enforcement agency that took your identity-theft report has contacted the agency that arrested the criminal. With your photo and fingerprints, you should be able to prove who you are—and who you're not. Your investigator should help you to recall any warrants that may have been issued in your name.

If they have found the real perpetrator, the agency can replace your name with his or hers. If not, ask them to replace your name with "John Doe." Ask the law-enforcement agency to indicate in the records and warrants for the real criminal that your name is not an alias, but rather that you are an identity-theft victim. Ask your investigator to prepare a *clearance letter* on the agency letterhead and a *certificate of release* to show that you were a victim of fraud.

Make several copies of these documents. Carry them with you so that if you are stopped by police and they incorrectly pull up your name from databases, you can set the record straight on the spot.

Ask the agency that issued the warrant which county, state, and federal agencies it reported the arrest information and what court issued the warrant. Also ask it to send notification to those agencies of the errors and to send you copies of the notification. Ask for the contact information for each agency that received the information and write a letter with a copy of your clearance to each one (return receipt requested) asking for an acknowledgment of the correction in their files.

Legal Lingo

A **clearance letter** is a formal statement by law enforcement that you have been cleared of any charges of wrongdoing. If you have been arrested, a **certificate of release** is documentation from law enforcement that you have been released from custody and are cleared of any charges. In some states like California you can get a **certificate of innocence** from a court that declares you "factually innocent" and a victim of criminal identity theft. In some states, such as California and Ohio, you can register with the attorney general's office as a victim of criminal identity theft so that if you are stopped and a warrant comes up, the officer can access the database to get verification of your innocence.

Don't rely solely on the bureaucratic agencies to make all the corrections; they are overwhelmed and understaffed. Although you are innocent and it's not your fault, protect yourself by following up to make sure the records are all corrected.

District Attorneys or Federal Prosecutors

If a case against you is in progress or if there has been a trial or a plea bargain, you'll need to contact the *district attorney* or *federal prosecutor* handling the case as well as the defense attorney for the perpetrator. You can find this information in the court filings.

Legal Lingo

The **district attorney** is the main prosecutor for the state in a given geographic region. A **federal prosecutor** is the equivalent of a district attorney for federally prosecuted crimes.

The law-enforcement agency that made the arrest (it could be local police for a state crime or the FBI or Secret Service for federal crimes) will have the contact information for the attorneys involved.

If the case already went to trial and the impostor was convicted, you'll need the entire court file. Call the original prosecutor if available (or the prosecutor's office if the prosecutor no longer works there, which happened to one of my clients) and provide all the documentation of your innocence. Ask the prosecuting office to prepare a motion to the court to clear your name from the case. If the prosecutor's office is overwhelmed, it may tell you that you will have to hire a private attorney. This could be very expensive, so I strongly suggest that you speak to the managing district attorney and ask for help, because you were a victim. In some cases they will assign a public defender to help you. If not, see Chapter 18.

Correcting Court Records

If criminal charges against your impostor have gone to court, whether the fraudster bothered to show up or not, you have a serious problem. You need a copy of the entire court file. You'll find out the court in your background check, or through law enforcement. The court records are disseminated to state and federal agencies and myriad commercial data brokers, so you must take correction procedures very seriously.

The court documents will indicate the name of the prosecutor including address and phone number and also let you know if the perpetrator was defended by a private lawyer, a public defender, or himself or herself. You'll need to first contact the lawyers involved and provide them the evidence of your innocence and the criminal's impersonation of you. If the criminal had legal counsel, that person should be able to help you to engage the district attorney's office. I have had good luck getting reputable prosecutors to make a motion before the court to clear the victim and issue a court determination of innocence.

The judge hearing the motion will be more inclined to rule quickly in your favor if the prosecutor is directly asking the court to correct the records. If you get an ethical DA, after he has substantial evidence and files a motion, he may be able to take care of the situation more informally with the court without your having to attend the hearing. Once the records are corrected, however, you still aren't finished with the courts. You'll need to contact the court administrative offices for the contact information of all governmental agencies and commercial entities that either access or buy the data relating to the court's dockets and

Information = Power

Should the district attorney be unwilling to help, contact the office of the attorney general of the state in which the crime occurred.

rulings. Ask how the court communicates corrected records to the entities; request a copy of the correction. It's important to always get written confirmation of any correspondence of any entity that corrects records with your name.

Governmental Databases and Commercial Data Brokers

Unfortunately, even clearing court records can leave you with a blemish on your name. Information brokers are not always careful about how current the information is in the records they keep and sell. I had one client who cleared his name of a fraudulent murder charge only to learn that brokers continued to list him as a murderer even after the courts had cleared his record.

That's why you need the contact information of all the governmental entities and agencies that receive the corrected arrest records and court documents. At the very least, write to the governmental agencies and confirm that they have corrected the records. Then, it's vital to run your own background check after about six months to see if the false records are still appearing. If you have made good friends with your local law-enforcement agency, you may be able to again ask them to run a criminal check on your name to see what comes up. If not, run your criminal background check to see what is reported. You also have the right to get your public records at no cost from www.choicepoint. com once a year. There are identity-monitoring companies like ID Watchdog.com that will also run a criminal check of your name and Social Security number for a fee.

It's also wise to contact the FBI (www.fbi.gov) to see if your name is identified with the perpetrator's fingerprints. The NCIC, which is the national FBI database, uses fingerprints for identification and matching, but court records often use the name and Social Security number.

If you find at any point that your name is still tarnished, call and write the data broker reporting the false criminal record, provide the documents of fraud from law enforcement or the courts indicating that you are innocent of the charges, and then demand that they investigate and correct it and provide you with the source of the information. Then work your way back to the source and dispute the errors. If information companies have out-of-date information on you, ruining your reputation, you may have a very good legal case against them since they have a duty to correct and maintain accurate consumer records under FCRA, so see Chapter 18.

If you are concerned about having to pass a screening by an employer or government agency, conduct your own background check done before you authorize the employer to do one. If you are a victim of fraud, let the employer know before you consent to a background check and ask for a copy. Also check the leading search engines with your name in quotations to see what comes up.

The Least You Need to Know

♦ Criminal identity theft is the most challenging to correct.

♦ If you are the victim of any type of fraud, run your own background check on yourself.

♦ Contact local law enforcement and file an impersonation report, asking the investigator for help.

♦ Get local law enforcement to take your live fingerprint scan and digital photo to compare with the real perpetrator.

♦ Obtain a clearance letter or certificate of release.

Chapter 16

Facing a Suit or Lien

In This Chapter

- ◆ Researching your status with the courts
- ◆ Handling suits and judgments
- ◆ Facing actions by the IRS or state tax authorities

Chapter 15 discusses what is perhaps the worst case of identity theft: when you are made to look like a criminal. But having to deal with civil court—whether a lien, a lawsuit, a judgment, or even a bankruptcy in your name—can also be traumatic. Using the approaches to fixing financial fraud and dealing with courts will help you challenge the wrongful actions and clear your name.

Get the Lay of the Land

You may have learned of the problem in a number of ways, including any of the following:

- ◆ A lien or judgment appearing in your credit report
- ◆ A notice from a lawyer or court

- A notice from your bank

- A notice from the IRS or other government agency

To address any of the above issues, you need to start with all of the information you can get. You should immediately respond, first by phone, if possible, and then by letter, to the person or place that made you aware of the problem. For example, if you get a letter from a lawyer or a notice from a bank, immediately call the person who sent the letter or other listed contact and get as much information as possible.

The first step to see what is happening is to go through your credit reports, as Chapter 4 explains. Look for either judgments or liens in the public records section, or any collection accounts that could have preceded a judgment.

Information = Power

You may be able to catch items before they turn into a lawsuit, judgment, or lien. Look for collection accounts that may precede the legal process. Check the credit header section of the credit report for any addresses that are not yours, because the fraudster may have sent misdirected notifications. Immediately dispute those addresses to the credit bureaus and find out who reported them. Also look at the inquiry section to see what entities have accessed your credit report and contact them to find out why.

There are two types of legal actions that may affect you: civil suits and government actions. If judgments or liens appear on your credit report, dispute the items as fraudulent with the CRA immediately in writing as you would for any other type of financial fraud under the FCRA, as Chapters 4, 5, and 6 explain. Even if the CRAs investigate and notify the reporting entities and the entries are removed from your credit reports, you still have work to deal with the problem directly so the difficulty doesn't come back to haunt you.

Personal Civil Cases

In a personal civil case, someone or some entity is suing you for some wrong done by the fraudster. It might be a creditor who issued credit to the fraudster, who didn't pay the bills. It could be for your impostor's breach of contract in a business dealing done under your name. It could be for a personal injury resulting from some negligent action taken by your impostor, like an automobile accident. It could even be a judgment of child or spousal support if your impostor married and had children using your identity and subsequently left or divorced.

As a result, someone is suing you and may even have obtained a *judgment* or a *lien*. An engineer victim called me after he was sued by a company that allegedly hired his impostor to design a building that failed.

> **Legal Lingo**
>
> A **judgment** is the decision or opinion by a court that determines a disputed matter. If there is a judgment against you as the defendant, you are ordered to pay or do some action (like fulfill a contract) in favor of the plaintiff(s) who sued you. A **lien** is a court order giving a person or company a legal interest in your property as security for a debt owed.

You're Sued or Threatened with a Suit

If a company or lawyer threatens that it intends to sue you, you've just received good news. Things are still in a state where, by proving the identity theft, you have a chance to convince the company or person that you are not the culprit and to either not file or dismiss an action with the court.

Once you learn of the intended lawsuit, immediately contact whoever notified you by phone to explain the situation. Follow up with a letter, return receipt requested, with your identity-theft report, FTC affidavit, copy of your driver's license, and all other pertinent evidence. Request, pursuant to FCRA 609e, copies of all documents and proof of their claim against you.

You should be able to resolve this without an attorney, but make sure that you get a letter from the entity that threatened the legal action, notifying you that your fraud claim has been accepted and no further action will be made and your credit report will be corrected. If you're told the case is dismissed, get a copy of the filed dismissal and check back later with the court's online website to be sure that the records reflect that the case shows the dismissal.

A Court Judgment Against You Exists

You will learn of a lien or judgment already entered with a court in one of four ways:

- As an entry on the public-records section of your credit report
- From your employer in the form of a wage attachment
- From your bank in the form of funds taken from your account to satisfy a lien
- Directly from the court

Contact the court clerk where the judgment was entered or the lien filed. Call first to get the case number and all particulars about how to obtain the entire file. Ask the court clerk to give you the name and contact information of the plaintiff's attorney who brought the action, as well as the identity-thief's attorney, in the unlikely event that there was one.

Next, send a letter documenting the conversation—including copies of the law-enforcement report, affidavit, and your driver's license—to the court and the plaintiff's attorney. Call the plaintiff's attorney and explain the circumstances and request copies of all the paperwork on the case.

Unfortunately, the attorney may not wish to help you because it is not in his or her best interest. No matter what, get the court filings online or contact the court for how to get the filed documents. Be aware that not all documents will be in the court's possession. For example, such discovery documents as depositions and interrogatories are not filed with the court. Depending on where the suit was filed, you may bring or send your identity-theft report and evidence of your identity to the judge to have the case against you dismissed. Ask the judge's clerk what action you may take to remedy the situation.

If the plaintiff's attorney is unwilling to assist you to correct the judgment or remove the lien, you may need to hire legal counsel in the
jurisdiction where the case was filed. Depending on the circumstances
of the fraudster's activities, the suit could have been filed in virtually
any state. You may have to travel to take the necessary action. Call the
local bar association in the court's jurisdiction and ask for a referral
for a lawyer experienced in the type of case before the court; if it is a
credit-card company, for example, you will need a consumer lawyer
experienced with FCRA and identity theft. If it is a child-support matter, ask for a family-law attorney who also understands identity theft.

Identity Crisis _____

Deal directly with the attorney who filed the case and don't try
to speak with the person or company directly. In fact, the company probably will refer you to the legal counsel who handled
the case, who would know the situation the best. A reputable,
professional attorney will more easily understand the situation. At the
very least, he or she will know the necessary steps to follow to rectify
the situation. An ethical attorney will inform the company or person who
brought the suit of the fraud and go to court to dismiss you from the
case.

If the plaintiff is unwilling to drop the action, even though it is clear
that it has been wrongly brought against you, you must contact the
court clerk and the judge in charge of the case with all the information. Explain that you are wrongly identified as the defendant. In such a
circumstance, you may need to hire a lawyer who understands identity
theft and the issues of the case. You may also have a cause of action
against the plaintiff for its own negligence in suing and causing you to
incur attorney fees and other costs and damages.

Tax Liens

A tax lien is an extremely serious problem. The IRS files what is called
a Notice of Federal Tax Lien when it thinks that you owe taxes and that
you don't intend to pay them voluntarily. The tax lien is a legal claim
to your property either as payment or as a way to secure payment for
your alleged tax debt. It serves as a public notice in court records and

on your credit report to other creditors that the government has a claim on your property.

The law requires the IRS to notify you in writing not more than five business days after the filing of a lien. However, if the fraudster who owes taxes to the IRS has given his or her address, you may not get the notice. You may ask an IRS manager to review your case. If that doesn't resolve things, you can request a Collection Due Process hearing through the IRS Identity Protection Specialized Unit (1-800-908-4490).

When writing the agency, submit a copy of your valid government-issued ID, such as a Social Security card, driver's license, or passport. Include a copy of your identity-theft report as well as a completed form 14039, *IRS Identity Theft Affidavit*, which you can get at www.irs.gov. Send the documents using one of the following options:

Mailing address:
Internal Revenue Service
P.O. Box 9039
Andover, MA 01810-0939

Fax:
1-978-247-9965

Ask the IRS to release and remove the lien and to notify all consumer-reporting agencies of the fraud so that the lien will be deleted from your profiles. After proving that you were not the one who owes the IRS debt, the IRS should release the lien.

Be sure to get the notice of the release of the lien in writing, and send that to the credit-reporting agencies to expedite the deletion of the lien from your credit profile. Obviously, if the IRS refuses to remove the lien, you will need to hire a tax lawyer and appeal the denial.

Bankruptcy

It's surprisingly common for identity thieves to file bankruptcy under their victims' names. I have heard from many victims who were shocked that their own credit cards were cancelled because their identity clones filed bankruptcy in another state. The thieves do so when they buy a house in your name and can no longer pay the mortgage, and filing bankruptcy stops all foreclosure proceedings. A fraudster renting an apartment can't be evicted while bankruptcy is in process.

If this has happened to you, report the fraud to the nearest *U.S. Trustee Program* field office. You can find it on the Internet (www.usdoj.gov/ust/eo/ust_org/region_websites.htm) or in a local telephone directory.

By federal statute, the bankruptcy court is a neutral party that represents the public interest. Thus, U.S. Trustee staff cannot directly represent the victim, but can give him or her steps to follow to remedy the situation. My experience is that the staffs often work with the victim to obtain information necessary for enforcement actions.

Legal Lingo

The **U.S. Trustee Program** is part of the Department of Justice that monitors the conduct of bankruptcy proceedings and the parties involved in them.

Depending upon the circumstances of the case and the procedures preferred by the Bankruptcy Courts in the local jurisdiction, actions by U.S. Trustee staff may include any of the following:

◆ Make a motion to dismiss a pending case in which the bankruptcy filer used a false name and/or Social Security number. In that case, ask that the U.S. Trustee also request the court for a specific finding that the named person did not file the case or authorize the filing, and that the signature was a forgery.

◆ Make a motion to expunge or void a pending or closed case. In that circumstance, ask that the case file be corrected and sealed as well.

◆ Make a motion to correct the true debtor's Social Security number in the bankruptcy court record, if you find out the name of the fraudster.

Ask the bankruptcy court to provide a list of whom it notifies of its dismissal or corrections. Follow up with those agencies, sending them copies of court documents clearing your name. You should have already disputed the bankruptcy as fraud on your credit reports for the CRAs to investigate. Although the public records are supposed to be updated by commercial information brokers and reported to the consumer reporting agencies, it is still important for you to provide a letter and documentation to the credit-reporting agencies as well to expedite the deletion process and protect yourself if the data brokers fail to update the records.

Be aware that although you would have seen your credit reports and should have already disputed the bankruptcy as fraudulent, if the court records verified the bankruptcy, the CRAs would not have deleted the bankruptcy until you proved the fraud to the court.

The Least You Need to Know

- ◆ If you are threatened with a lawsuit by anyone, deal with it immediately.

- ◆ If a lawsuit was filed, contact the court and the plaintiff's attorney where the suit was filed to get the complete case file.

- ◆ If bankruptcy was filed in your name, contact the nearest U.S. Bankruptcy Trustee Office where the action was filed.

Chapter **17**

Cyber Identity Theft

In This Chapter

- ◆ Understanding cyber identity theft
- ◆ Tracking down the service that the criminal uses
- ◆ Stopping the activity and getting the identity of the criminal

So far I've been discussing the theft of your real-world identity. But the rush of Internet technology has left the "virtual you" vulnerable. Cyber identity thieves can take over your online identity or create a new you on the web to further their illegal plans. Unfortunately, because the online world has been developing at such a clip, the ability to steal identities races ahead and the law hasn't kept up.

There is no well-recognized approach to stopping a case of cyber theft, but this chapter has a series of steps that should help you battle the problem, and restore your good name.

Cyber Identity Theft Is Real

You may have become the victim of *cyber identity theft* in a number of ways. Someone might impersonate you on a social networking site to embarrass you as a form of revenge. Hackers might take over your computer to send spam or perform attacks on other computers using your *IP address*. Or the person might trick you into revealing the user-ID and password for your online account or use more typical identity-theft techniques to take over your account, or create a new account, e-mail address, blog, or website in your name. Businesses find out that thieves create fake websites or clone a company's website to intercept traffic and start taking orders and credit cards from customers who think they're dealing with the real business.

Legal Lingo _____

Cyber identity theft occurs when someone impersonates you online. It can be for financial gain, to commit other crimes, or to get revenge. Except when the fraudster uses your Social Security number online to create financial accounts and get into your bank, it's possible for someone to commit cyber identity thefts with relatively little personal information about you. The **IP address** is the identifying number of your connection to the Internet.

You will usually find out about cyber identity theft in a very negative way. You may be contacted by an angry stranger who read something your impostor wrote on a blog or on a website, allegedly by you, which put your reputation in jeopardy. Your impersonator might have written a threatening e-mail to your boss. Some of the horrendous cases I've dealt with included a victim having strange men show up at her apartment requesting sex as a result of provocative invitations created by her impostor revealing the victim's home address and private phone number; an e-mail address created in the name of an ex-spouse by her former husband, threatening to kill their children so he could use the material in court to win custody; and a victim who learned that his profession as a psychologist was used by a former student to create a website to give online counseling sessions for a fee.

To address the problem, you must first find the information. Do a web search of yourself with your name in quotes, such as "Mari Frank" or "Mari J. Frank". Don't limit your investigation to one search engine, as each one indexes the Internet differently. Dogpile (www.dogpile. com) will bring you the top combined results from Google, Yahoo!, Bing, and Ask.com, and so can save you time. Also, check the "images," "news" and "newsgroup" directories available on individual search engines as well.

Once you have evidence of your stolen identity, call your local law-enforcement agency and ask for the high-tech crime unit. You'll need to complete an FTC affidavit and file a report with law enforcement. But first I must warn you that law enforcement usually won't want to give you a report because it is unlikely that they will have the resources to investigate this labor-intensive crime unless there are many victims, or if money laundering or terrorism might be involved.

In that case, just ask for an informational identity-theft report. Tell them you need the report to send to the Internet service providers so that they will help you take false entries off the net and assist in the investigation. With the police report, the completed affidavit, government-issued identification, and other information about your own Internet service provider, contact the service provider that your impostor is using.

Going to the Source

Generally speaking, someone impersonating you on the Internet is using some service provider to create a personal profile, host a website, or provide e-mail service, so you will need to contact that service provider.

Identity Crisis

When a hacker takes control of your PC without your knowledge and sends out spam, or gets into your actual computer with so-called spyware, your problem is within your own system. In that case there will be no service you can track. Instead, take your computer to a technician, explain the problem, and have the professional remove all viruses and spyware. You will need to set up appropriate hardware and software protection to keep intruders out. Learn more at http://www.firewallguide.com/.

In the case of a fraudulent profile on a social-networking site, the company that runs the site is the provider. However, finding the service provider that runs a given website takes a bit of research:

1. Look at the URL—the address that starts with "http://" and ends with something like ".com" or ".biz". Isolate the domain name—the part that looks like "name.com".

2. Point your browser to www.internic.net. Look for the "Whois" link on the front page and click it. Fill in the form using the domain name you have from the site.

3. The site will give you the name of the ISP, or Internet service provider that hosts the site. Now you go to the ISP site and again look for the Whois link.

4. Fill in the form using the domain name. You will get a contact record for the person or company that owns the domain.

Don't get too excited in advance. It's possible to anonymously register a domain so the contact information of the owner does not appear, and it's also not unheard of for people to provide phony contact information. But at least you know who the ISP is and, if luck is with you, you will have contact information for the fraudster. Don't contact the fraudster yourself; let law enforcement or the ISP deal with the impostor. Ask the ISP to remove the fraudulent information from the web.

Finding the owner of an e-mail address is a similar investigation. The part that comes after the @ sign is the domain. However, it is possible to send e-mails in such a way as to make it look as though it came from one address when it actually came from another. Get a technician to help you look at the *header* of the e-mail in question. If the person used *IP spoofing*, it will likely be very difficult if not impossible to find from where the e-mail actually came. However, the use of any technique to disguise the true origin of an e-mail is strong proof that you were not the one who sent it.

> **Legal Lingo**
>
> The **header** is a part of an e-mail that carries the origin and intended destination as well as various other types of control and status information. **IP spoofing** is a technique by which people hide their real connection locations on the Internet and make their transmissions look as if they came from elsewhere.

Investigating the Fraud

When you ascertain the service provider, look up its contact information on its website. You may have to send an e-mail asking for a street address. If someone has taken over an online account of yours or created one in your name, then use the steps I gave you in Chapter 8 for handling fraud that doesn't appear on your credit reports.

Contact the company and explain the fraud and that you need two things: to have the fake "you" taken off their system, and to get the original application and all evidence of the fraud in their electronic files.

You will need to follow up by mail, return receipt requested, with a copy of the law-enforcement report, the affidavit, a copy of a government-issued ID, and a copy of a utility bill to confirm your identity. Explain that you did not authorize the use of your name and that the account must be closed immediately. Also say that under the Fair Credit Reporting Act, section 609(e), you demand that the service provider send all the correspondence and documentation for the account, including the contact information and IP address for the person who opened it, and that a copy of this information should go to the law-enforcement agency listed in the report.

I won't lie to you—this situation does not exactly fall under the FCRA, but the only source of your rights as a victim of identity theft is in the FCRA. I have used this procedure with clients and we have gotten the information without a subpoena. Remember you are trying to assert your right to end someone misusing your name. Because there is no legislation specifically giving you cyber-identity-theft rights per se, you will be asserting a way to deal with the mess authorized by federal law. The more legal protocol you can point to, the more companies and authorities will follow your lead.

The reason you want the name or IP address of the actual fraudster is to stop the impersonator from simply moving to another service and using your good name again. Once you have an IP address or a name, contact the police in that location and make a formal complaint.

Do not contact the identity thief yourself unless you know the person and he or she is not violent. In that case, ask the person to cease and desist. You may have a right to a civil action against that person for defamation or some other cause of action depending on the facts. Consult a lawyer about the issue.

Additional Help

Cyber identity theft can be difficult to fight and you may need some additional tools and allies. Here are some that may be of help, depending on the exact circumstances.

Digital Millennium Copyright Act

The *Digital Millennium Copyright Act of 1998* was not created to fight cyber identity theft. But if your business has found that someone is impersonating it, the DMCA may provide additional leverage for you to get what you need to take down fraudulent information.

> **Legal Lingo**
>
> The **Digital Millennium Copyright Act of 1998 (DMCA)** is a law focused on electronic and online use of copyrighted materials.

Under the DMCA, copyright owners have the right to demand that ISPs take down websites that display their materials without permission. Virtually any attempt to create a phony business site will involve using images and text from the materials of the real business, which means copyright infringement.

Ask the service provider, or check its site, for details on how to issue a DMCA takedown notice. Here are the elements you will need to put into the notice (and note that the specific language is important):

- A statement saying that you are the owner of an exclusive right that is being infringed

- Identification of the work or, if multiple works, a list of the works

- Identification of the web pages that are infringing your copyright, including the URLs

- Your contact information, including mailing address, telephone number, and e-mail address

♦ A statement that you "have a good-faith belief that use of the material in the manner complained of is not authorized by the copyright owner, its agent, or the law"

♦ A statement that the information in the notification is accurate, and under penalty of perjury, that you are authorized to act on behalf of the owner of an exclusive right that is allegedly infringed

♦ Your signature

Service Providers and Industry Groups

Many service providers understand the problems of cyber crime, fraud, and identity theft, and offer help to consumers who have found themselves victims. For example, eBay has a link for hijacked accounts with instructions on what to do.

There are also industry groups that help consumers and member corporations deal with cyber crimes, including identity theft. The APWG (www.antiphishing.org) does research into phishing, the practice of tricking people into revealing personal information by e-mailing them and pretending to be a legitimate institution. The Messaging Anti-Abuse Working Group (MAAWG, www.maawg.org) and Digital PhishNet (DPN, www.digitalphishnet.org) are two others.

Specialty Law Enforcement

A number of metropolitan areas have an identity-theft task force. One will typically include representatives of local law enforcement, a Social Security Administration inspector, a postal inspector, and sometimes an IRS inspector. They usually also have high-tech crime investigators who know how to investigate all sorts of computer crime and who may be able to provide help in this emerging area of cyber identity theft.

If you live in or near a large metropolitan area, your own local law-enforcement agency may also have a high-tech crime unit that has the skills and tools to help ferret out the online criminal.

School Districts

Both cyber identity theft and cyber bullying have become a significant problem in schools. It may involve students or even teachers. If your child is the victim of cyber identity theft, in addition to the other actions in this chapter, go to the local school district, starting with the principal of the school, and ask for assistance. Cyber identity theft among young persons is usually by someone they know from school. If the principal doesn't help you, call the administrative offices and find out who deals with these issues; they often have dedicated resources to address them.

Journalists and the Media

Sometimes the only way to get help from the authorities is to turn up the heat. That client of mine who was harassed by strange men could not get help from the New York City police to even take a report until we got the story on the front page of *The New York Times*. Once local attention started focusing on what she was going through and the lack of law-enforcement cooperation, the police miraculously took the report and investigated and we stopped the impostor. I wouldn't suggest this as a first step, but when all else fails, it is surprising what some media attention will do.

Technology Help

Unless you are a computer forensic analyst or a real techie yourself, it will be tough for you to resolve the cyber identity theft. Enlist high-tech law enforcement, Internet service providers—and even the FBI computer crime division—to help you if this is an especially invasive case. Computer forensics professionals are experts; hiring them can be expensive, so as a victim, get as much evidence as you can to bring to law enforcement to encourage them to investigate.

The Least You Need to Know

◆ Cyber identity theft can target individuals or businesses.

◆ Before you file a report with law enforcement and fill out an affidavit, search online for your name to gather as much evidence as possible.

◆ Track down the service provider for the domain name.

◆ Engage service providers to send you documentation of the fraud under FCRA 609e.

Chapter **18**

If Worse Comes to Worst

In This Chapter

- ◆ Learn to work the system to your benefit
- ◆ Get help when you need it
- ◆ Put a public spotlight on those who won't help

Your circumstances may be so complex, or involve such thorny legal problems, that tackling them on your own would be self-defeating. Sometimes a company, agency, or a particular person decides to be unreasonable and unsympathetic and refuses to cooperate, no matter how the law stands on your side. I remember one corporate in-house investigator who had finally agreed that my client was a fraud victim, but he stubbornly refused to reopen the case and admit his initial mistake.

Sometimes you may find yourself dealing with someone who simply doesn't understand the severity of the crime or his or her responsibilities, either legal or ethical. A company may ignore your letters and pretend not to have received them or tell you they were lost. Many companies refuse to send the documents of the fraud as required by the FCRA because they don't want to admit their carelessness in issuing credit. Unfortunately, although the company is in violation of the law, you don't have a private right to sue them for not sending the documents.

Now is when you must become creative and find ways to get the resolution you need. This chapter looks at what you can do through persuasion, gentle confrontation, escalation of the issue, and the use of professional help. But you must stay calm while focusing on what you *must* accomplish without letting your anger take over.

Making Them Listen

In today's litigious society, people often assume that a full-out legal battle is the only way to resolve issues. As I mentioned, there are some limits to your ability to even sue negligent creditors and credit bureaus since the Fair and Accurate Credit Transactions Act created victim rights, but disallowed a right to sue under many of the provisions. For that reason, many times creditors just ignore victim rights, knowing that, unless a federal agency gets involved, they can ignore certain provisions of the law.

But the good news is you can negotiate your way to success more easily than you would imagine. As an attorney and mediator, I've often seen high-quality settlements without filing a lawsuit. To successfully remove the roadblocks and recover your identity, the most important tool you can use is persuasion, backed by knowledge of your rights and clear, organized, written evidence to back up your assertions of fraud.

It's always best to first attempt to resolve all issues without a threat of further action. Try to enlist aid from companies and organizations by helping them to understand that being of assistance to you is actually the right and smart thing to do for themselves as well. But be ready to also help them understand that if they refuse to resolve the issues, you will be persistent and will be forced to escalate your concerns to higher levels.

Information = Power

If a company or organization's employee doesn't understand the responsibilities under the law, ask to speak to a supervisor. If that person is also in the dark, fax specific pages of this book or pages from the FTC.gov/idtheft website to them to explain the necessary steps required to investigate and assist you. Often procedures or statements in print bring the "power of legitimacy" to your statements. Many victims have gotten help by just letting the companies know that the advice was in my books.

When you speak to law-enforcement investigators, remember that they may have hundreds of cases on their desks. The more evidence you bring them in a concise and organized manner, the more likely they will be to help you and investigate further. A chronological, bullet-point history of the major issues with names, phone numbers, and dates will be easy to read and understand. A cover note with a list of numbered documents attached will provide your investigator with an uncomplicated format to use to put time into the case.

When you make your initial calls to place a fraud alert with the credit bureaus, you will not get a human being. Rather, you will provide your sensitive information to an automated recording. A week or so later, you will receive a return letter with a case number informing you of your right to receive your free credit report and other rights. Once you receive your credit report, you'll be given a case number and a phone number to call to speak with a live person. Before you call, be sure to write out any questions you have and be sure a copy of your credit report is in your hands. For example, you may need contact information for creditors listed in the inquiry section of your report, or you may not understand certain data on the report.

The most challenging communication may be with creditors who stand to lose money due to fraud. The fraud investigators want to be heroes for their companies, and they have many files on their desk. They have an incentive to deny your claim, and many won't be as sympathetic as you'd wish them to be. When you call the fraud department, ask for the employee's full name (they may only give you a first name; if so get the employee number and city where he or she is located), title, an e-mail address (if available), a fax number, and a snail-mail address.

Be very courteous, no matter how abrupt the answers. If the conversation is being taped (you will hear notice of it), it's a good idea for you to tape it as well. In fact most of the time upon answering the phone, the automated voice will say "this conversation will be taped for quality assurance." That announcement gives you the right to also tape the conversation; don't record unless you hear first that the entity is recording. And keep any recording you make, since it may have great relevance later if they deny your claim.

Information = Power

You can find inexpensive recording devices that connect to your phone at stores like Radio Shack.

Clarify your situation, and that you wish to send them your FCRA-compliant documents and ask if anything else is needed to clear your name. Assure them that you know they are busy and probably have quite a few cases, but let them know of your taxing circumstances, too. Be cooperative, but persistent. If they are disagreeable, ask to speak to a manager. If they refuse, get the name and phone number or employee number of the supervisor and call back.

You may be very frustrated by a lack of sensitivity and willingness to help you. But showing that you understand your rights under the law can help gain cooperation. For example, the Red Flag Rules of the FCRA require all creditors and financial institutions to develop written procedures for preventing and mitigating identity theft. So ask the fraud investigator to please provide you a copy of the written identity-theft policies under the FCRA Red Flag Rules they are required to implement to help victims like you.

Be respectful but assertive. Let them know that you have this book in your hand and that you are aware of your rights. You must resolve your fraud case and get your life back. Ask them to be mindful that if you are able to resolve this with them, you will be forced to escalate the issue. (More on that later in this chapter.)

As is true virtually everywhere, information is power. That's why it's so important to know what your rights are, ask for what you are entitled to, and retain copies of your letters, sent return receipt requested. It's also critical to scan in the return receipts into your computer so that you have evidence that the companies received the letters you sent.

This one piece of evidence has helped me to positively resolve cases by proving the bad faith of some companies who had told my clients that they never received their FCRA-compliant letters.

Getting Free Resources and Help

One way to support your efforts is to access the free resources available. Here are some of the major ones:

♦ The Federal Trade Commission provides vast free information about identity-theft protection, laws, and resources at www.ftc. gov/idtheft (or call at 1-877-IDTheft).

♦ The Identity Theft Resource Center is a non-profit agency that provides fact sheets, guides, protection measures, additional resources, and phone and e-mail help. Its website is www. idtheftcenter.org, and toll-free victim assistance number is 1-888-400-5530.

♦ Privacy Rights Clearinghouse, a non-profit, privacy-oriented entity providing fact sheets, additional resources, and other great information, can be found at www.privacyrights.org.

♦ World Privacy Forum, a non-profit dealing with Medical Identity theft at www.worldprivacyforum.org.

♦ The U.S. Department of Justice provides free information on how to deal with fraud and investigation at www.usdoj.gov/criminal/ fraud/websites/idtheft.html.

For a much more complete list of free resources, see Appendix B.

Escalating the Discussion

When you're not having success with one person at a company, ask to speak to the supervisor. If you are told that the person is not available, ask for the name and contact information to use (including e-mail or fax if possible) to send a letter outlining your concerns. Always keep copies for yourself, explaining what happened with the previous person with whom you spoke.

If you are told that that you cannot have the name of the supervisor, ask for the executive services department phone number and contact information. If you hit a dead end, go on the Internet and search for the company and find the "Investor Relations" pages. There you will find the name of the top executives and the address. You may write to the "top dog" and let them know of your challenges and ask for help. Also copy your letter to the regulators for the industries and make a complaint to the Federal Trade Commission at www.ftc. gov/idtheft.

Information = Power

When contacting a corporate CEO, indicate that you are copying your letter to the regulator of the company's industry. For example, for national banks (not credit unions), you will write to the Comptroller of the Currency. It raises the seriousness in the company's eyes. Just as an underling doesn't want attention from the boss, the company would not want an investigation by federal regulators.

You'd be surprised at the number of times the office of the head of the organization will look into a matter, only to have the staff take a renewed interest because they are advised to "make this issue go away."

Commercial Identity-Theft Prevention and Rehabilitation

A number of commercial services and products can help you regain your good name. ID Analytics has a free online program that will score your risk of identity theft through a statistical analysis of such things as your name, Social Security number, phone number, date of birth, and address. It has tips on how to keep your identity from being stolen—or keep it from being stolen again, causing you to immediately repeat everything you have just done.

My own website is Identity Theft Prevention and Survival (www. identitytheft.org), with dozens of pages of free education, resources, and guides, as well as information about my other books and educational materials. We provide e-mail and telephone guidance (1-800-725-0807), representation, expert testimony, training, and consulting.

You've probably heard advertisements from companies claiming to be able to completely protect your identity by "locking" or "freezing" your credit report. But as you saw early on in the book, this is easy to do yourself and costs nothing. As far as seeing what is new in your credit report, know that, in addition to the two free credit reports, you are entitled, as a victim pursuant to federal law (some state laws entitle you to more), to a free copy annually from each of the CRAs, as well as your free public-records search and other specialty consumer reports from companies like ChoicePoint. Here's a partial list of the reports you can get for free annually:

C.L.U.E. Reports for home & auto insurance:

- ChoicePoint C.L.U.E. Reports: ChoiceTrust.com or 1-866-312-8076.

- ISO Insurance Services A-Plus Reports: ISO.com or 1-800-627-3487.

MIB medical report:

- Medical Information Bureau: MIB.com or 1-866-692-6901.

Tenant reports:

- ChoicePoint: ChoiceTrust.com or 1-877-448-5732.

- SafeRent: 1-888-333-2413.

Check writing reports:

- ChexSystems: ConsumerDebit.com or 1-800-428-9623.

- Shared Check Authorization Network: ConsumerDebit.com or 1-800-262-7771.

- TeleCheck: 1-800-209-8186.

There are also identity restoration services that say they can help you recover your identity. This works by your giving their fraud resolution staff a limited power of attorney to act on your behalf. Most of them only deal with financial identity theft. You will need to provide them your sensitive data, including your SSN, credit-card numbers, and credit reports, and trust that they will protect that information. Because the facts of the fraud are really known only to you, you will still be heavily involved in the process. I have consulted with some very reputable companies in this area that have helped victims to resolve their identity-theft issues. But before you agree to pay for any of these services, read the fine print in any guarantee. The warranty may actually state that they will spend the equivalent time of a million dollars at some undisclosed rate per hour, rather than give you the funds. Some companies do offer you identity-theft insurance that reimburses you for out-of-pocket costs, time off from work, and limited attorney fees if you are sued.

To find out more about the various identity rehabilitation services, visit the non-profit Consumer Federation of America (www.consumerfed. org) and read the report "To Catch a Thief: Are Identity Theft Services Worth the Cost?" Also look at the resources in Appendix B to compare services and make up your own mind. Also visit www.ftc.gov/bcp/edu/pubs/consumer/idtheft/idt05.shtmand and read "To Buy or Not To Buy: Identity Theft Spawns New Products and Services To Help Minimize Risk."

When Overwhelmed, Get Legal Help

Unfortunately, sometimes your efforts, or the labors of reputable identity-theft services, will not get the results you need. There are also times when the issues are thorny enough—identity theft during divorce or custody cases, criminal identity theft, problems with the IRS, medical identity theft, or very complicated financial fraud—where you can't depend on a do-it-yourself approach.

At such times, you should consult an attorney who is experienced dealing with identity-theft laws. Call your local bar association and ask for a consumer lawyer who deals with the Fair Credit Reporting Act, if it is a financial issue; or a criminal lawyer for criminal identity theft; a medical-privacy lawyer, if it deals with medical identity theft; or a tax lawyer for tax issues.

You can also visit the website of the American Bar Association (www. abanet.org/premartindale.html) or the National Association of Consumer Advocates (www.naca.net) to find an attorney who specializes in consumer law, the Fair Credit Reporting Act, and the Fair Credit Billing Act. Also see Appendix B of this book for other legal resources.

Getting a legal consultation doesn't mean you must bring a lawsuit. That is the action of last resort, because it could be expensive if the lawyer will not take the case on *contingency*, and time consuming if companies continue to delay and stall. I suggest you get a legal consultation to gain knowledge and insight about how your specific facts relate to the situation and what options you should consider. Many times victims call me and I help them create a strategy that helps them recover their identity and resolve the issues of settlement without my having to take the case. Remember, knowledge is empowering.

Legal Lingo

Contingency means that the lawyer takes a fee as a percentage of what you obtain from either a suit or settlement, usually with out-of-pocket expenses (like depositions and court costs) paid by you up front or off the top of the money from your recovery. If you don't win your case, you don't pay the lawyer any fees but you may be liable for costs. Read your potential lawyer's retainer-fee agreement carefully and ask clarifying questions before you sign.

Don't delay if you can't get the credit bureaus to delete the fraud or if the creditors violated the law. Under the Fair Credit Reporting Act, you must file a lawsuit within two years after you discover that a company or credit-reporting agency violated the law, but no later than five years after the violation first occurred. See an attorney within at least a year of your first letter to the CRAs or the creditors if they fail to remove the fraud from your records.

If your case involves egregious violations of the FCRA, a lawyer may be willing to work on a contingency basis.

Ask the lawyer what types of identity theft cases he or she has handled and if written opinions of his similar cases are available for you to review. Check out the attorney's website and visit the state bar website to see if there are any complaints against the attorney before you call for an appointment.

When you meet with the attorney about your case, bring a concise bullet-point history of the events of your identity theft. Bring copies of all the paperwork, including your notes and victim chronology, police report, and FTC affidavit as well as correspondence with all the companies. Never give anyone your original documents—make sure you keep those.

Negotiation, Mediation, or a Lawsuit

Be aware that the process of a lawsuit will be time consuming and at times uncomfortable. You will be forced to re-experience all of the pain as you are interrogated in depositions, spend time cooperating with your attorney, lose time from work preparing, and maybe find yourself at your physician's office due to the stress. It's stressful on your family and may be a challenge with your work schedule. A court-filed case is a public record, and all the information (hopefully your Social Security number and sensitive data should be redacted in accordance with court rules) becomes available to anyone, including another identity thief. At the same time, if a company has badly injured you and compounded the wrong by not stepping up to its legal obligations, then you may wish to find ways to recover your losses.

Hidden Agenda

Your negotiation power is based on the leverage you have. If you have good evidence, you are a credible witness, you have a legitimate and worthwhile case with compensable damages, and your attorney is articulate and prepared, most reputable companies will seek to settle fairly rather than risk a big loss and bad publicity.

The first approach I always use is negotiation. You of course may have already tried this yourself; however, an experienced lawyer has the arsenal of the law to hopefully bring the opposing party to its senses rather than its knees. If you have kept copies of your e-mail, written, and recorded correspondence showing evidence of an organization's unwillingness to investigate, you might have enough ammunition to make it worthwhile for the company or entity to settle at the negotiation stage and avoid public knowledge.

Your lawyer will help you value the case and understand the issues. To help you understand how your case is valued under FCRA, you'll need to be able to show that you have sufficient damages to make it possible for the attorney to take the case, on contingency, against large companies with ample funds to pay their attorneys to engage in a long-term court battle. Your damages will include such things as an inability to get a car or home loan, credit refusals, loss of a house, a job, or bank funds, and proof of emotional distress. The types of violations for a high-value case would include a credit bureau's failure to correct credit reports and a creditor's failure to properly investigate after a bureau provides notice of fraud.

The higher the value of a case, the more likely that companies will engage in negotiations to avoid a public trial. A negotiated settlement will usually include a confidentiality clause in which the company will require that you keep the terms of the settlement confidential and not discuss what happened any further. In some very egregious cases, in which my clients have been very wrongly treated and the companies have acted in bad faith, refusing to negotiate fairly, those clients have spoken to the media. If you are very articulate and honest, and the truth is embarrassing to the company, you may gain an advantage and settle early and positively.

If negotiation fails, mediation is another alternative you can use either before or after a lawsuit is filed. This is a facilitated negotiation in which a neutral third party, usually a lawyer or retired judge, facilitates the process of settlement so that the parties reach a confidential agreement in a written settlement. Mediation is usually less stressful and less expensive than litigation, but both parties must agree to engage in the process. Other benefits are that it is private, usually faster, and confidential. This protects the privacy concerns of all the parties.

Publicly Exposing Bad Behavior

You may not have a high-enough valued case to make it feasible for a lawyer to accept it on contingency, or the violations in your case may not allow for a private lawsuit; for example, if a creditor ignored your fraud alert and issued credit to an impostor, or refused to give you copies of the evidence of the fraud. You may feel victimized by the company that caused the problem, and frustrated by its uncaring attitude and lack of redress.

Thousands of victims share your dissatisfaction, which is why it's so important to make the circumstances known publicly so that changes will take place to better protect consumers and help victims to recover more quickly and easily. An important tool in getting satisfaction can be exposing the bad behavior of careless companies in the media, or blogging about what happened to you. I have seen miraculous turn-abouts in company cooperation after victims speak to the media or blog about what happened in a respectable, credible manner on websites like ConsumersUnion.com.

No one likes bad press—especially big public companies. I strongly suggest that you only tell the facts of your case. Truth is an absolute defense against a claim of defamation. Contact television stations, radio stations, and newspapers, and succinctly tell your story to an editor or consumer reporter, explaining that what happened to you can happen to anyone and it's important to protect the public from the poor treatment of victims.

Contact IDTheftCenter.org, PrivacyRights.org, IdentityTheft.org, or ftc.gov/idtheft to share your story, and volunteer to speak to the media. These websites are often contacted by the media to see if victims are willing to tell their stories. Just be careful. If you have any skeletons in your closet, it's best to lie low, since the media attention could be uncomfortable. If you are willing to write an article or letter to the editor of your local newspaper, your voice can be heard. Once the article is published, you may send it to the company, the company regulators, the Federal Trade Commission, and your legislators. The key is to be very professional, concise, and articulate.

Calling and Writing Legislators

Another source of help and public disclosure is notifying your state and federal legislators. Contact your state and federal representatives and explain the situation. Ask for help and find out if they can suggest a state committee for you to write. You will most likely speak with a staff person and not the elected official, but you can write a letter. Also, you can find out the names and e-mail addresses of members of financial services committees at the state and federal levels and apprise them of the challenges for victims. You may wish to copy the letter to the company who has wronged you, and the federal regulators as well. A call from a legislator's office can add pressure for a positive resolution.

Don't Get Mad, Get Busy

If you're reading this book and still having a problem with a company or an agency, you're probably furious and frustrated, and your family and friends are irritated from hearing your complaints. Stop complaining and take action. Use your anger to motivate you to speak out for what is fair. If this is happening to you, I guarantee you are not alone. Thousands of other victims experience such aggravation and feelings of defeat. There are about 10 million new identity-theft victims a year, so don't isolate yourself. Be a savvy leader and make some positive changes for yourself and others.

The Least You Need to Know

- ◆ Be polite but assertive when persuading companies and agencies to help you resolve your identity theft.

- ◆ Escalate to higher authorities if you aren't getting a reasonable response.

- ◆ Inform state and federal agencies, officials, and even the media to increase pressure on companies to do the right thing.

- ◆ Interview qualified lawyers who have experience with your type of case and get a consultation even if you don't want to file a lawsuit.

- ◆ Negotiation and mediation are good alternatives to a lawsuit.

- ◆ Make anger your ally.

Chapter 19

After the Storm

In This Chapter

◆ Working effectively with police, prosecutors, and the courts

◆ Knowing your rights as a victim in court

◆ Protecting yourself from future identity theft

At this point, you've gone through much of what you must do to recover from the identity theft. You're likely still dealing with the CRAs, the creditors, and possibly one or more government agencies. Nearing the end of your ordeal, the last thing you want to think about is reliving the entire experience. And yet, that's what you need to do to really get beyond it.

Most victims would like the definitiveness of knowing who did this to them. That is not always possible. The most important outcome is not getting the bad guy; it's recovering your good name and sanity back to normal. But what if the person does it again to you, or sells your sensitive data to someone else who victimizes you again? What if the thief proceeds to the next injured party?

You may find closure if you are one of the lucky ones who can bring the perpetrator to justice. If so, you need to know how to handle yourself in the pursuit of justice. You also need to take proper steps to protect your identity going forward. This chapter will lead you through the court system if the crook is caught and show how to feel more secure in the future.

If They Catch the Thief

Most identity thieves remain unknown, free to wreak damage to you or someone else. But sometimes your own investigative work in conjunction with the compassionate efforts of law enforcement will catch your evil twin.

If your impersonator is apprehended, although you may be worried about the perpetrator's vengeance, there are some good reasons to cooperate in the prosecution:

◆ You've been violated and you are helping to make the criminal accountable for his or her crimes. This process will be an incentive for him or her to stop repeating the crime against you and others.

◆ Your assistance to the court and the criminal justice system empowers you to no longer feel like a victim but rather a defender of truth, which might facilitate emotional closure.

◆ You have the right to ask the court to order restitution for your out-of-pocket costs and lost wages.

◆ If there are companies or agencies that don't believe you are a victim of fraud, the fact that you assisted in prosecuting the perpetrator will offer additional evidence of your innocence.

If you have reached the point where the prosecutor has even decided to file a complaint against your impostor, you should be proud, because that means you have cooperated with law enforcement and provided the DA or federal prosecutor with enough evidence for them to move forward. Without your facts and substantiation, there would be no case.

If the prosecutor decides to press charges, you need to know what to expect so that you can be calm and prepared. Here are some things you need to know about:

◆ Victim-impact statements

◆ Victim's rights

◆ Victim assistance

◆ Restitution

These are all components of the last stages of being a crime victim: relief.

Victim-Impact Statement

Depending on how strong the evidence is or how much time from the court's violent crime schedule is left for economic crime, the prosecutor might offer the criminal a *plea bargain*. In such circumstances, you will not need to testify in court, but you will need to talk to the probation department since they are usually involved in the plea bargain. You will have the right to ask for restitution and give the judge a *victim-impact statement*.

A well-written, concise victim-impact statement is critical to the judge at sentencing time because it helps the court to understand the severity of the crime and how your life has been affected. Economic crime is often perceived to be only about money, but if you have handled your case as recommended, you should not be paying the bills that your impostor created. Your real damages may be time, effort, reputation, and emotional.

Legal Lingo _____

A **plea bargain** results in a somewhat reduced charge or sentence recommendation in exchange for a guilty plea. A **victim-impact statement** is usually a written communication (sometimes also oral if the victim is available or the judge allows a video statement) from the identity-theft victim to the judge, detailing the emotional, physical, financial, and other impacts, stresses, and problems resulting from the actions of the identity thief.

The statement is sent to the judge before sentencing or before agreement to a plea bargain. Many states specifically require the court ruling on the offender's status to consider the victim's statements in making its decision. It gives the judge good reason to consider what you have suffered in the sentencing. Many judges, used to hearing cases of violent crimes such as murder, rape, and armed robbery, may not understand the consequences of a stolen identity. So it's your job to enlighten the court so that justice may be accomplished.

Your impact statement should address the heart of what you and your family experienced as a result of being victimized by this crime. Be brief and succinct. Explain how you spent hours calling and writing letters, dealt with unsympathetic companies, lost your job, fought with your spouse, lost sleep, lost your appetite or gained weight, experienced post-traumatic stress disorder, got an ulcer—whatever you experienced. Speak from your heart but be very specific. You have a right to describe your losses and what you think should happen to the perpetrator. Here are some things you might consider requesting of the judge (although he or she is not obligated to fulfill your requests):

◆ Restitution for your losses with an accounting of such out-of-pocket losses as lost wages, travel costs, postage, long-distance charges, and attorney fees, with detailed written explanations and documentation.

◆ Long-term probation for the impersonator, if you know the person or you believe that this person is remorseful and could be rehabilitated.

◆ Mandatory counseling for the impostor and perhaps drug rehabilitation if the impostor is involved in using drugs.

◆ An appropriate jail or prison sentence for the criminal, especially if this person is a repeat offender or has multiple victims.

Along with victim-impact statements at sentencing, most states also allow input at the parole hearing of the offender. As a victim, you will be required to maintain a current address on file with the parole board, the prosecutor's office, or criminal-justice agency. The original victim-impact statement that was prepared for the sentencing hearing is often included in an offender's file by corrections and paroling authorities, and reviewed as part of the parole process.

The right to present victim-impact information, whether written or oral, is usually guaranteed by law. It will be important for you to speak with the prosecutor or his office to discuss how and when you must present your statement. Ask the prosecutor to refer you to the victim-assistance program so you can get help in preparing your impact statement and your testimony, if needed.

Information = Power

Whenever you send a victim-impact statement to the judge, send it out one to two weeks before either the beginning of the trial or the sentencing hearing. That will give the judge time to receive and review it. It's crucial that you send it in a timely manner or you will lose your right to restitution.

Your Rights as a Victim

If your impostor has not been able to secure a plea bargain, then he or she will go to trial. If the proceeding is out of state or a long way from your home and there is plenty of evidence against him, you may not need to attend trial. You would still have the right to send an impact statement. For many victims, the prospect of testifying in court may be unsettling or even scary.

It's important to know that the prosecutor represents the state, not you. For that reason it's important to ask for help from the victim-assistance office, which is usually within the prosecutor's office. Ask the victim-assistance program or the prosecutor for a written explanation of your rights within the jurisdiction of the court. Here are some of the rights you are entitled to expect:

- ◆ To be reasonably protected from the person who is accused of stealing your identity.

- ◆ To request that sensitive information—including Social Security number, bank accounts, credit report details, and driver's license number—be redacted from any documents that will be filed with the court.

- ◆ To receive notification of all court hearings.

- ◆ Unless the court determines that your testimony would be affected by what you heard, to attend the trial and hear evidence.

◆ To speak to the prosecutor and the investigators and provide them evidence.

◆ To get copies of all information about the trial, including the complaint, the hearings, the transcripts (you will need to pay for this), the sentencing, and plea bargains.

◆ To be heard by the judge either orally or in writing in a victim-impact statement, including what you think should happen to the perpetrator

◆ To have the court consider ordering restitution be paid to you in a timely manner

◆ To be free from unreasonable delays in the prosecution of the case

◆ To fairness, respect, and privacy

Identity Crisis

Although you have a right to be in court, you must be respectful of the judge and attorneys, even if you don't agree with what is said—or the sentence.

Victim Assistance and Probation

When working with the prosecutor assigned to your case, the process may seem confusing and even frightening. Most district attorney or federal prosecuting attorney offices have victim-assistance programs that provide counseling to victims and help prepare them for the various stages of the trial. To find out more about victim assistance, visit the National Office of Victims of Crime online at www.ojp.usdoj.gov/ovc.

The probation department will investigate the defendant to make a recommendation to the court regarding the possibility of a probation sentence by the court. The probation department will interview the defendant, the victim, and others who may know the defendant and make a recommendation for or against probation. Once probation is ordered, either instead of or after incarceration, a probation officer will hold the person convicted of a crime accountable to ensure that he or she is meeting the requirements of the probation. A person "on probation" has been convicted of a crime but has served only part of the sentence in jail, or has not served time at all.

Restitution

In your victim-impact statement, you can ask the court to order the thief to make restitution to you for such things as the following:

♦ Medical expenses

♦ Therapy costs

♦ Lost wages

♦ Expenses such as travel costs and child care to participate in the trial process

♦ Lost or damaged property

♦ Prescription charges

Information = Power

Restitution will not cover such things as pain and suffering or emotional distress, but may cover reasonably expected future losses, such as ongoing medical or counseling expenses.

In calculating the restitution owed, a court will look at the victim's losses and the convicted person's financial resources. Be aware that your impostor may also be ordered to pay restitution to the credit-card companies and others from whom he has stolen.

This is one reason it's critical to keep logs of all your expenses, as Chapter 2 explains. Realistically, if your impostor stole your identity for financial gain, it is unlikely that he or she will have the means to pay restitution. If the impostor goes to jail, it is likely that you won't get restitution while he or she is incarcerated unless they are earning wages in prison.

Many jurisdictions provide that restitution orders become civil judgments, which means that, as a victim, you may eventually be able to collect, because the orders can remain in effect for a long time, typically 10 to 20 years. Depending on the jurisdiction, and whether the fraudster has the funds, your civil judgment may be enforceable immediately or after the criminal-justice process—probation, prison, or parole—is complete. When payment of restitution is a condition of probation or parole, probation or parole may be revoked if the defendant willfully fails to pay.

The reality is you can't count on receiving restitution, even if the court orders it, and you may need to emotionally let go, because chasing the money may not be worth your time, effort, or stress. What's most important is your physical, financial, and emotional health. So once you have resolved all the outstanding issues of your identity-theft adventure, you are ready to set up barriers to protect yourself as best you can from future fraudsters.

Protect Yourself

When you have finally accomplished the tremendous feat of regaining your good name, whether it is clearing all the fraud from your credit reports, your medical records, your criminal file, your governmental records, or all of the above, you should feel relieved that the arduous journey has ended.

Now, with all your awareness of the fragility of your identity, you need to create an action plan to safeguard all that you have regained. To that end, here are some things you can do to protect yourself going forward.

Review Consumer Reports

Federal law entitles you to two free credit reports in the year of your victimization; in some states, like California, you are entitled to one a month for 12 months. You are also entitled to get your free annual report from each of the three major agencies at www.annualcreditreport.com.

You probably have written for your seven-year fraud alert, telling potential creditors not to issue credit without calling you first at the number you designated (cell phone). You may even have written to the credit bureau for a stronger security freeze, as Chapter 4 describes. You may wish to sign up for a credit-monitoring service, which will alert you to any changes in your credit report.

Information = Power _____

Some employers offer free credit monitoring as a benefit, and some organizations you join will provide this as an additional free benefit. I suggest that, if you do purchase a monitoring service, it should include all three major CRAs and include your credit score as well. Some companies offering credit-report monitoring are also including Internet monitoring, public-records monitoring, criminal-database monitoring, and identity-theft insurance. Compare them all and consider if any of the products fit your needs and your budget. Just remember, much of what they do you can do at no cost, but there is a time factor.

You also have rights to other free annual consumer reports under the FCRA. It's a good idea to take advantage of getting your free disclosure of those as well:

- Reports on insurance claims, employment work history, and tenant history from ChoiceTrust.com (see Chapter 8); tenant history from SafeRent (1-888-333-2413); ISO Insurance Services A-Plus Reports (ISO.com or 1-800-627-3487)

- MIB medical report of medical insurers of claims in your name (see Chapter 14)

- Check-writing reports (see Chapter 7)

- Personal reports, including public records, from ChoicePoint (see Chapter 8); ChoiceTrust (www.choicetrust.com); and LexisNexis (www.lexisnexis.com/privacy/for-consumers/request-personal-information.aspx, or 1-888-332-8244)

Cancel Your Debit Card

Debit cards—the ones with the MasterCard or Visa logo printed on them—are dangerous because thieves can use the card without the PIN, online or by phone or fax, to commit fraud. Get an ATM card to get cash from an ATM machine or check your balance. You are safer using a regular credit card as long as you pay your balance each month.

Keep Your Information Safe

Do not share details of your identity or life with people who don't need to know the information. Keep financial data, your Social Security number, and other critical information at home in locked filing cabinets. Shred any financial, confidential, and sensitive documents you discard.

Review All Your Financial and Medical Statements

When you get monthly billing, bank, or investment account statements, scrutinize them for activity that could be signs of identity theft. Examine statements of benefits that come from healthcare insurers to see if the details are correct.

Secure Computers and Wireless Broadcasts

Whether a desktop, laptop, PDA, or smartphone, put a password on the device and encrypt the contents, so if stolen, the thief won't be able to read what is on the machine. Install and use firewall and anti-virus software.

Properly configure home network routers to use encryption and install security systems like firewalls. Don't transmit personal, financial, or confidential data that isn't protected.

Identity Crisis

Cell phones are particularly vulnerable, because people talk on them freely in public places and share sensitive information without considering the lack of privacy. It is easy for people to eavesdrop on your conversation, or for professional criminals to listen to communications. Be careful what you transmit. Don't keep sensitive data on your cell phone unless it is encrypted.

Take Care When Paying Bills

If possible, don't use checks at all. Your account number and routing number on the bottom of your check can be copied and printed by fraudsters to create checks on software purchased at any office store. The checks are not reviewed by the bank and the money is gone from your account before you know it.

If you must use a check, use a gel ink pen that cannot be acid-washed by fraudsters, who are known to erase the name of the recipient and change it to the fraudster's name. Instead of sending checks out for payments from your home mailbox where they can be stolen, use the post office.

Better yet, use electronic online banking (making sure to secure your computer and to use complex passwords) and make payments from your own bank electronically to pay monthly bills.

Give Yourself a Privacy Audit

Go to Google.com and sign up for a "Google Alert." Enter your name in quotes and ask for a free e-mail alert when your name comes up on the Internet.

There are many things you can do to protect your identity and also to be more private. Develop a privacy consciousness. You may wish to get my book *Safeguard Your Identity: Protect Yourself with a Personal Privacy Audit*. In it, I give you hundreds of easy things to do to set up barriers to protect your privacy and identity.

In our society, no matter how careful you are, myriad companies and agencies have your Social Security number and complete profiles—including your bank, credit-card companies, health insurer, doctors, accountants, educational institutions ... the list goes on. If they allow access to an unscrupulous or negligent employee, or if a hacker or burglar steals that information, that's beyond your control. But the good news is that now you know the clues. You know how to intervene early, what steps to take, and you are empowered to guard your life. You may have been victimized, but you are not a casualty. You are wiser for the triumph!

The Least You Need to Know

- ◆ Partner with law enforcement and prosecutors to help bring the thief to justice.

- ◆ Prepare a concise victim-impact statement to submit to the prosecutor for the court to review before sentencing.

- ◆ Review your victim rights and ask for restitution and a reasonable sentence for the thief.

- ◆ Let go of any obsession to collect restitution if your impostor has no funds or if he goes to prison; just get your life back and move on.

- ◆ Review your free credit reports and other specialty reports once a year.

- ◆ Review billing, bank, and healthcare statements immediately to catch any signs of fraud.

- ◆ Secure your personal, confidential, and financial information offline and online.

- ◆ Do your own privacy audit and safeguard your identity.

Appendix A

Glossary

account takeover   A form of credit-card or bank fraud in which the criminal charges purchases to someone else's financial accounts or takes over financial accounts to extract or transfer funds.

accounting of disclosures   A list of persons or institutions that received a consumer's consumer report or healthcare information from the healthcare provider, the dates on which disclosures happened, details of the information shared, and reason for sharing the information.

application fraud   A form of credit-card or bank fraud in which the criminal uses a consumer's identity without permission to establish new accounts, unbeknownst to the consumer.

certificate of innocence   A document issued from a court in certain states that declares you "factually innocent" and cleared of charges.

certificate of release   Documentation from law enforcement that you have been released from custody and are clear of any charges.

Check 21   A federal program that allows banks to transmit electronic images of a deposited check for payment rather than shipping the original paper version.

check verification company   A business, considered a consumer reporting agency under FCRA, that collects information about returned checks and reports that data to its merchant customers.

child identity theft   The unauthorized use of a child's personal identifiers for an illegal purpose.

clearance letter   A formal statement by law enforcement that you have been cleared of any charges of wrongdoing.

collection agency   A company that buys unpaid credit accounts from the original creditor and then attempts to collect payment from the consumer.

contingency fee   When a lawyer's fee is a percentage of what the client obtains from either a suit or settlement, usually with out-of-pocket expenses (like depositions and court costs) paid by the client upfront or off the top of the money recovered.

credit history   Part of the credit report showing creditors' reports about the payment history of the consumer's accounts with them.

credit-reporting agency (CRA)   A consumer reporting company that collects credit information on consumers and sells that information, in the form of credit reports, to other companies, landlords, lenders, potential employers, and others. The three main CRAs are TransUnion, Experian, and Equifax. There are also many resellers of credit data.

credit reports   Compilation documents kept by credit reporting agencies that show current and former accounts, who inquires about your credit record, and data about which entities have granted credit in your name.

creditor   A company that extends credit to a consumer or business.

criminal background check   A document that shows the arrests, warrants, convictions, jail time served, and probation that a person has undergone.

criminal identity theft   When a thief uses someone else's identity when arrested for a crime other than identity theft.

cyber identity theft   When someone impersonates another online.

Digital Millennium Copyright Act of 1998 (DMCA)   A U.S. law focused on electronic and online use of copyrighted materials.

dispute   A notification to a creditor by a consumer that specific information in a credit report or on an account is fraudulent and alleged to be incorrect.

district attorney   The main prosecutor for the state in a given geographic region.

Dunn & Bradstreet   A company that tracks credit and payments of businesses.

Electronic Fund Transfer Act   A law that was established in 1978 that provides a number of rights to consumers regarding *electronic funds transfers.*

electronic funds transfer (EFT)   The computer-based banking system for electronic billing and payments

extended fraud alert   A fraud alert requested in writing that can stay on credit files for up to seven years.

Fair and Accurate Credit Transactions Act (FACTA)   Amendments to the *Fair Credit Reporting Act* that address duties of credit reporting agencies, creditors, and others to consumers regarding identity theft and other issues.

Fair Credit Billing Act   The Fair Credit Billing Act is a law, passed in 1986, that changed the Truth in Lending Act to "protect the consumer against inaccurate and unfair credit billing and credit card practices."

Fair Credit Reporting Act (FCRA)   A U.S. law intended to govern the accuracy, fairness, and privacy of information in the files of credit reporting agencies.

Fair Debt Collection Practices Act   A U.S. law that governs how debt collectors can attempt to collect payment from consumers.

federal prosecutor   The equivalent of a district attorney for federally prosecuted crimes.

Federal Trade Commission   A federal agency that enforces consumer-protection laws regarding lending, credit, debt collection, and identity theft. Its mission is to prevent unfair competition and unfair or deceptive acts or practices affecting commerce.

Financial Industry Regulatory Authority (FINRA)   An independent regulator for securities firms doing business in the United States.

financial statements   Periodic summaries of an account, including credit cards, bank accounts, and insurance policies.

fraud alert   A notation that tells anyone receiving your credit report that you're the victim of identity theft and not to issue credit without calling you first at a specific number.

FTC identity-theft affidavit   A form to be completed by victims that alerts companies to your identity-theft scenario and is required to be submitted to clear your name.

Gramm-Leach-Bliley Act (GLBA)   A federal law requiring, among other things, limited privacy protections against the sale of consumer financial information.

hard-pull inquiry   A company's request for a credit report initiated by a consumer or the consumer's impostor seeking to open an account or get a loan or a job.

header   In credit reports, the part with the consumer's name, address, and other personally identifying information. In an unrelated meaning, in e-mail, the header is the part that carries the origin and intended destination as well as various other types of control and status information.

Health Insurance Portability and Accountability Act of 1996 (HIPAA)   A federal law that governs how healthcare entities deal with patient information and operate with regard to paper and electronic records.

health savings accounts (HSAS)   Savings accounts with special tax benefits that are available to people who enroll in high-deductible health insurance plans.

ID theft complaint   Notification to an entity by a consumer who has obtained a law-enforcement identity-theft report that specific information in a consumer report or on an account is fraudulent and alleged to be incorrect.

identity theft   The unauthorized use of your personal identifiers for an illegal purpose, usually for profit, a benefit, or revenge.

Identity Theft Resource Center A non-profit organization devoted to the prevention and recovery of identity theft.

identity-theft report A document, created by a local, state, or federal law-enforcement agency, providing official notice that you are the victim of identity theft.

initial fraud alert A fraud alert that stays on your credit file for up to 90 days and can be placed by phone.

inquiry sections Parts of the credit report showing requests for profile information that is part of a regular review of an account and requests from potential new creditors to see the credit file.

IP address The identifying number of your connection to the Internet.

IP spoofing A technique by which people hide their real connection locations on the Internet and make their transmissions look as if they came from elsewhere.

judgment The decision or an opinion of a court that determines a disputed matter.

lien A court order giving a person or company a legal interest in your property as security for a debt owed.

listing of benefits A document that shows what services, treatments, medicines, and devices the healthcare insurance carrier paid for on behalf of the patient.

marital settlement agreement A contract that divides property between two former spouses in a divorce case.

master log book A file that tracks every step of your identity-recovery process.

mediation A facilitated negotiation in which a neutral third party, usually a lawyer or retired judge, facilitates the process of settlement so that the parties come to an agreement.

medical identity theft The act of someone using another's identity to get healthcare in that person's name.

Medical Information Bureau (MIB)   A medical insurance databank that compiles consumer reports used by nearly 500 insurance companies in the United States and Canada.

National Crime Information Center (NCIC)   An FBI-operated computer-based compendium of criminal justice information.

notice of privacy practices   Written explanation of what information an entity collects, how it uses the information, with whom the information may be shared, how consumers may obtain their information, and how much it may cost.

personal earnings and benefit estimate statement (pebes)   A form that the Social Security Administration sends you to show the history of earnings it has on record for you by year and an estimate of the resulting future Social Security benefits.

plea bargain   In a criminal case, a negotiated reduced charge or sentence recommendation in exchange for a guilty plea.

postal inspector   A law enforcement agent working for the U.S. Postal Service.

power of attorney   The legal delegation of authority to another to act on the grantor's behalf

prior payment history   Part of the credit report that shows if the consumer was late in paying accounts as well as the amount and dates of the consumer's payments.

return receipt requested   A U.S. Postal Service letter option that requires the delivery person to obtain on a card a signature acknowledging delivery of the letter. The card is returned to the sender as proof of receipt and must be sent for all correspondence dealing with identity theft.

security freeze   A written request to a CRA that locks your credit file so potential creditors cannot obtain your credit profile in order to issue you credit without you providing a password to the credit bureaus to release the report.

Social Security Death Index   An easily obtained, regularly updated list of people that the Social Security Administration lists as having died. It includes the person's Social Security number.

Social Security inspector   A law-enforcement official with the independent auditing and investigative branch of the Social Security Administration.

soft pull   Either an account review of credit profile by a company with whom the consumer already has a relationship, or a review by a company to offer the consumer a pre-screened credit offer.

spousal identity theft   Identity theft perpetrated by a spouse.

substitute copy   A copy of the front and back of a paper check that can act as a legal replacement for the original.

synthetic identity theft   A fake identity created from personal information from multiple people or a combination of real and fabricated information. The ultimate victim is the one whose Social Security number is used.

Truth in Lending Act   A law requiring disclosure of credit terms and governing credit cards.

U.S. Trustee Program   A part of the Department of Justice that monitors the conduct of bankruptcy proceedings and the parties involved in them.

victim chronology   A running chronological history of your identity-theft experience, necessary for legal purposes if a lawsuit is to be filed later.

victim-impact statement   A communication, usually written although sometimes also oral, from the identity-theft victim to the court, detailing the emotional, physical, financial, and other impacts, stresses, and problems resulting from the actions of the identity thief.

Appendix B

Other Resources

Non-Profit Identity Theft Resources

CALPIRG (California Public Interest Research Group)
A research and lobbying consumer group that addresses identity
theft and consumer issues.
1107 9th Street, Suite 601
Sacramento, CA 95814
Phone: 916-448-4516
E-mail: info@calpirg.org
Website: www.calpirg.org

Consumer Federation of America
Association of 240 pro-consumer groups whose aim is to advance
consumer interest through advocacy and education.
1620 I Street NW, Suite 200
Washington, D.C. 20006
Phone: 202-387-6121
Website: www.consumerfed.org
email-cfa@consumerfed.org

Identity Theft Resource Center
Provides support and assistance to victims of identity theft.
Co-directors: Linda Goldman-Foley, Jay Foley.
P.O. Box 26833
San Diego, CA 92196
Phone: 1-888-400-5530
e-mail: itrc@idtheftcenter.org
Website: www.idtheftcenter.org

National Center for Victims of Crime
Refers victims of crime to local services. Provides counseling and
victim services. Publishes bulletins on various criminal topics.
2000 M. Street NW, Suite 480
Washington, D.C. 20036
Phone: 1-800-FYI-CALL or 202-467-8700
Website: www.ncvc.org

National Fraud Information Center
Consumer Assistance Service
Website: www.fraud.org

National Organization for Victim Assistance (NOVA)
Refers victims of crime to local victim assistance programs.
510 King Street, Suite 424
Alexandria, VA 22314
NOVA: 703-535-NOVA
Hotline: 1-800-879-6682
Website: www.trynova.org

Privacy Rights Clearinghouse
A non-profit consumer information, privacy protection, and advocacy
program.
Beth Givens, Director
3100 5th Avenue, Suite B
San Diego, CA 92103
Phone: 619-298-3396
Fax: 619-298-5681
Website: www.privacyrights.org

U.S. PIRG
U.S. Public Interest Research Group, the national lobbying office for
state PIRGs.
218 D Street SE
Washington, D.C. 20003
Phone: 202-546-9707
E-mail: uspirg@pirg.org
Website: www.pirg.org

Government Identity Theft Resources

Federal Citizen Information Center
Referral to appropriate agency
1-888-878-3256

Federal Communications Commission (FCC)
For cellular phone and long-distance fraud.
Consumer and Government Affairs Bureau
445 12th Street SW
Washington, D.C. 20554
1-888-225-5322
Email: fccinfo@fcc.gov
Website: www.fcc.gov

Federal Deposit Insurance Corporation (FDIC)
The FDIC supervises state-chartered banks that are not members of
the Federal Reserve System and insures deposits at banks and savings
and loans.
Division of Compliance and Consumer Affairs
Regional Offices
East 20 Exchange Place, 6th Floor
New York, NY 10005
West 25 Jessie Street at Ecker Square, Suite 2300
San Francisco, CA 94105
Washington, D.C. 20429
Phone: 1-877-275-3342
Website: www.fdic.gov

Federal Reserve System
The Fed supervises state-chartered banks that are members of the
Federal Reserve System.
Consumer Help Center
P.O. Box 1200
Minneapolis, MN 55480

Consumer Help Phone Number: 1-888-851-1920
Email: Consumerhelp@federalreserve.gov

Website: www.federalreserve.gov

The Federal Trade Commission
Identity Theft Clearinghouse
The Consumer Protection Mission of the FTC is to protect consum-
ers from companies that misinform or overreach with regard to our
economy.
Identity Theft Clearinghouse

Attn: CRC-240
600 Pennsylvania Avenue NW
Washington, D.C. 20580
Phone: 1-877-IDTHEFT (438-4338)
Website: www.consumer.gov/idtheft

Internal Revenue Service
9672 Via Excelencia, Building 101
San Diego, CA 92126

1111 Constitution Avenue NW, IR-7052
Washington, D.C. 20224

Tax Fraud Referral Hotline: 1-800-829-0433
Taxpayer Advocates Office: 1-877-777-4778
Website: www.irs.gov

Tax Fraud Referral Hotline: 1-800-829-0433
Taxpayer Advocates Office: 1-877-777-4778
Website: www.irs.gov

National Credit Union Administration (NCUA)
The NCUA charters and supervises federal credit unions and insures
deposits at federal credit unions and many state credit unions.

National Credit Union Administration
1775 Duke Street
Alexandria, VA 22314-3437
Phone: 703-518-6300
Consumer Assistance Hotline: 1-800-755-1030
Website: www.ncua.gov

Office of Comptroller of the Currency (OCC)
The OCC charters and supervises national banks. If the word
"national" appears in the name of a bank, or the initials "NA" of its
name, then the OCC oversees its operations.
Customer Assistance Group
1301 McKinney Street, Suite 3450
Houston, TX 77010
Phone: 1-800-613-6743
FAX: 713-336-4301
Website: www.occ.treas.gov

Office of Privacy Protection-California
Provides information for consumers and victims regarding California
and federal law.
Office of Information Security and Privacy Protection
1325 J Street, Suite 1650
Sacramento, CA 95814
Phone: 1-866-785-9663, 916-323-0637
Website: www.privacy.ca.gov

Office of Thrift Supervision (OTS)
The OTS is the primary regulator of all federal and many state-
chartered thrift institutions, which include savings banks and savings
and loan institutions.
Office of Thrift Supervision
1700 G Street NW
Washington, D.C. 20552
Phone: 202-906-6000
E-mail: publicinfo@ots.treas.gov
Website: www.ots.treas.gov

Social Security Administration
P.O. Box 17768
Baltimore, MD 21235
Website: http: //www.ssa.gov/oig/hotline/ssnmisuse.htm
To report fraud: 1-800-269-0271
To order Personal Earnings and Benefits Statement: 1-800-772-1213

U.S. Department of State
Passport Services
Consular Lost/Stolen Passport Section
1111 19th Street NW, Suite 500
Washington, D.C. 20036
Phone: 1-877-487-2778
Website: www.travel.state.gov/passport/lost.html

U.S. Postal Inspection Service
Criminal Investigations Service Center
Attn: Mail Fraud
222 S. Riverside Plaza, Suite 1250
Chicago, IL 60606
Phone: 1-877-876-2455
Website: postalinspectors.uspis.gov

U.S. Securities and Exchange Commission (SEC)
The SEC's Office of Investor Education and Advocacy serves investors
who complain to the SEC about investment fraud or the mishandling of
their investments by securities professionals.

SEC Office of Investor Education and Advocacy
100 F Street NW
Washington, D.C. 20549-0213
Phone: 202-942-7040
Website: www.sec.gov

U.S. Trustee (UST)
Contact the Trustee in the region where fraudulent bankruptcy was
filed.
Website: www.usdoj.gov/ust/
To report bankrupcy fraud, e-mail: ustp.bankrupcy.fraud@usdoj.gov

Or mail to:
Executive Office for U.S. Trustees
Criminal Enforcement Unit
20 Massachusetts Avenue NW, Suite 8000
Washington, D.C. 20530

Check-Verification/Check-Guarantee Firms

Certegy Check Payment Recovery Services, Inc.
P.O. Box 30046
Tampa, FL 33630
Phone: 1-800-437-5120
Fax: 727-570-4936
Website: www.certegy.com

Chexsystems

Attn: Consumer Relations
7805 Hudson Road, Suite 100
Woodbury, MN, 55125
Phone: 1-800-428-9623
Fax: 602-659-2197
Website: www.chexhelp.com

Global Payments, Inc.
10705 Red Run Boulevard
Owings Mills, MD 21117
Phone: 1-800-846-0626
Website: www.globalpaymentsinc.com

TeleCheck
Consumer Relations
P.O. Box 4451
Houston, TX 77210
Phone: 1-800-710-9898
Consumer Relations: 1-800-280-7196
Consumer Relations Fax: 402-916-8180
Website: www.telecheck.com

Consumer Reports: Information Brokers

Federal law allows all consumers to obtain one free specialty consumer report per year from major specialty reporting agencies. If someone has used your name and Social Security number for employment purposes, get healthcare, etc., you will not find that information on your credit report. It is a good idea to check these information brokers to see what information is collected and sold about you.

ChoicePoint
Prepares and maintains information on consumers for insurance, employment, and tenant history.
www.choicetrust.com or www.choicepoint.com
Consumer Assistance Center: 1-888-497-0011
Phone for free auto or homeowner's insurance report: 1-866-312-8076
Phone for free tenant history report: 1-877-448-5732
Phone for free employment background check 1-866-312-8075

Medical Information Bureau (MIB)
A nationwide specialty consumer reporting agency that collects, profiles, and maintains records concerning life, disability, and health information for insurance purposes.
Phone: 1-866-692-6901
Website: www.mib.com

Infoline@mib.com
Medical Information Bureau
50 Braintree Hill Park, Suite 400
Braintree, MA 02184

Credit Card Companies

American Express
Phone: 1-800-528-2122
Website: www.americanexpress.com

MasterCard Assistance Center
Phone: 1-800-627-8372
Website: www.mastercard.com

Visa Assistance Center
Phone: 1-800-VISA911 (Hotline)
Website: www.visa.com

Credit Reporting Bureaus

Free credit report for all consumers, once a year. To order your free reports from all three major credit reporting agencies once a year: call 1-877-322-8228 or visit www.annualcreditreport.com.

Equifax
Equifax Fraud Division
P.O. Box 740250
Atlanta, GA 30374-0241

To report fraud: 1-800-525-6285
To order copy of report: 1-800-685-1111

Experian (formerly TRW)
Experian Consumer Fraud Division
P.O. Box 1017
Allen, TX 75013
Website: www.experian.com

To report fraud: 1-888-397-3742
To order copy of report: 1-888-397-3742

TransUnion
To report fraud: 1-800-680-7289
Fraud Division
P.O. Box 6790
Fullerton, CA 92634
Website: www.transunion.com

To order copy of report: 1-800-888-4213

To opt out of pre-approved offers of credit for all three credit reporting agencies, call 1-888-5-OPTOUT (1-888-567-8688). This will stop the credit reporting agencies from selling your name and creditworthiness on promotion for five years. If you wish to opt out permanently, you must write to each of the agencies at the addresses above.

Legal Resources

FBI
Criminal Justice Information Services Division
J. Edgar Hoover Building
935 Pennsylvania Avenue NW
Washington, D.C. 20535-0001
Phone: 202-324-3000
Website: http: //www.fbi.gov/

FBI Internet Crime Complaint Center: 1-800-251-3221
Website: www.ic3.gov

Identity Theft Prevention and Survival
Attorney Mari Frank provides assistance to consumers and identity-
theft victims with resources, books, and legal assistance.
Mari J. Frank, Esq.
28202 Cabot Road #300
Laguna Niguel, CA 92677
Phone: 1-800-725-0807 or 949-364-1511
Fax: 949-363-7561
E-mail: contact@identitytheft.org
Website: www.identitytheft.org

National Association of Consumer Advocates
Organization of people who represent consumer victims of fraud.
1730 Rhode Island NW, Suite 710
Washington, D.C. 20036
Phone: 202-452-1989
Fax: 202-452-0099
E-mail: info@naca.net
Website: www.naca.net

National Consumer Law Center, Inc.
Provides case assistance and legal research. Provides representation for
low-income and community-based organizations.
7 Winthrop Square
Boston, MA 02110
Phone: 617-542-8010
Fax: 617-542-8028
E-mail: consumerlaw@nclc.org
www.consumerlaw.org

National Association of Attorneys General
Consumer Protection and Charities Counsel
2030 M Street NW, 8th Floor
Washington, D.C. 20036
Phone: 202-326-6000
Fax: 202-331-1427
Website: http://www.naag.org

MyFairCredit.com
Provides extensive legal information about identity theft and credit
reporting. Attorneys and firms listed are independent and dedicated
to using the Fair Credit Reporting Act to protect consumers suffering
credit reporting errors and identity theft.

U.S. Department of Justice
Identity Theft Information
Website: www.usdoj.gov/criminal/fraud/idtheft.html

Index

D

CHECK OUT THESE
BEST-SELLERS

More than 450 titles available at booksellers and online retailers everywhere!